10 April

The Life
and Destiny
of
Isak
Dinesen

We must leave our mark on life while we have it in our power, lest it should close up, when we leave it, without a trace.

—Karen Blixen

Vi maa præge Livet
mens vi har Magt over
det, at det ikke skal
lukke sig naar vi faer
ud af det, uden Spor. —
Rungstedlund Sept 1961.
Karen Blixen.

The Life and Destiny of Isak Dinesen

Collected and edited by Frans Lasson

Text by Clara Svendsen

The University of Chicago Press

Chicago and London

The University of Chicago Press, Chicago 60637
The University of Chicago Press, Ltd., London

Phoenix Edition 1976. Printed in the United States of America

International Standard Book Number: 0-226-46916-6

Library of Congress Catalog Card Number: 75-40669

ACKNOWLEDGMENTS

When the idea for this book about Karen Blixen, who was known to the world by her nom de plume, Isak Dinesen, arose, it seemed to me that the one person eminently qualified for the task of writing the texts to accompany the photographs would be Clara Svendsen, Karen Blixen's secretary for many years. She accepted my proposition, and the making of the book became possible thanks to her close co-operation as the indispensable cicerone at Rungstedlund, eagerly joining in the search for photos in attic rooms, drawers and boxes, while at the same time discussing with the editor of the pictorial materials current problems concerning the text. Certain photos appear in the book primarily because Clara Svendsen had a special story to tell in connection with them. The greater part of the photos are published here for the first time.

Karen Blixen's heirs and the Rungstedlund Foundation have granted the editors free access to the photographs contained in Karen Blixen's private files. Without this generous courtesy it would not have been possible to give the book its present size.

The Royal Library of Copenhagen, where Karen Blixen's unpublished manuscripts, as well as other "Blixeniana," are kept, has given us invaluable help. In this connection, special thanks must be extended to Mr. Kaare Olsen, head of the manuscript department, and the library's eminent photographer, Carl Gerli. I am also deeply grateful to Mrs. Kirsten Scheel Hartvigson for her untiring aid and assistance in working out the index of names.

Last but not least I would like to thank Karen Blixen's brother, the author Thomas Dinesen, V.C., who has shown an inspiring interest in our work on the book and who has contributed some of the best photos of Karen Blixen in her African environment, which were taken during his visits to the farm in the 1920's. These photographs from the life of Karen Blixen represent many personal memories of Thomas Dinesen's; they bear witness to one of the most sensitive and mutually rewarding relationships between a brother and sister known to Danish literature.

F. L.

For permission to quote from the works of Isak Dinesen I am indebted to Random House, Inc., in the United States, and to Putnam & Co. Ltd. and Michael Joseph Ltd. in Britain.

C. S.

INTRODUCTION

One could have wished for Karen Blixen that she had had the opportunity of sitting for Sir Joshua Reynolds or had had her features preserved for eternity by the malicious and brilliant precision of a Toulouse-Lautrec. It would have matched the style in which she herself demonstrated absolute artistic power in her later and mature years, when she gave her contemporaries a grandiose and very consciously composed picture of herself which simultaneously confirmed and enlarged the readers' impression of the author of *Seven Gothic Tales*. However, Karen Blixen, known to the literary world as Isak Dinesen, became famous in a time when the art of drawing or painting the human face had irretrievably degenerated while the photograph made triumphant progress everywhere. The few painted portraits existing of her either reproduce the model's external pose or the popular and banal image of Isak Dinesen as a mysterious and romantic storyteller, but say nothing about the radiance and the shadows of her many-colored personality.

Although the Dinesen family often and willingly had themselves photographed—and thus there exists a large number of photos from Karen Blixen's childhood as well as from her years in Africa—photography as art or documentary did not seem to interest her seriously until the time when she returned to live at Rungstedlund. It was a time when what she considered her true life had ended and she was once again living in her mother's house, where, imposing upon herself an incredibly strict self-discipline, she realized the unfulfilled but never forgotten literary dreams of her youth. At that point the photographs of the family and the African highland became visible proof of the reality which she had now left behind, but even so she refused to accompany the description of her African life with photographs, despite the fact that innumerable books of travel were then being photographically illustrated. And of course she knew exactly what she was doing. Her book had no need for pictures, seen through the lens of a mechanical receiver. Each vision in *Out of Africa* was rooted in a deeper reality than the photographical; each was interpreted through the eyes of an artist and etched by the passion of a poet.

As long as she lived Karen Blixen was extremely reluctant to open drawers and family albums to a public eager to know the matter-of-fact world behind the apparent reality of her books. The reason for this reluctance may have been that she wished to preserve the at once intimate yet reticent relationship with her readers, created by her book about the years in Africa. But another reason was probably that a publication of the family photos would have meant that the most painful experiences of her life, which she had always kept out of her books, would have had to be mentioned. The death of her father by his own hand, the unrequited love of her youth, her wrecked marriage and the incurable disease which was the tragic result of this mistake, these were all such painful experiences that she could barely mention them to her most intimate friends, and she felt that only with great difficulty could   13 they fit into the overall image of her fate. If the truth was to be revealed, it must be told outright. Karen Blixen herself realized that much in her outlook on life as well as in her attitude towards other people was incomprehensible without a knowledge of those crucial experiences. And as an artist she instinctively sensed what such an insight into the high stakes of the game and the deeply personal background of her particular philosophy of destiny might mean for the assessment of her works. But the hour to speak out did not come during her lifetime.

Only now, seven years after her death, do we begin to make out more than the contours of her life, one of the most tragic of any Scandinavian writer. Parmenia Migel's biography, *Titania*, will be known to American and English readers. Monographs by such initiated experts as Aage Henriksen and Robert Langbaum have placed Karen Blixen's figure and writings in a wider psychological and historical framework than was apparent during her lifetime. These studies as well as Aage Kabell's distinguished first-hand inquiry into the biographical background of the stories have laid the foundation for true scholarly research of Isak Dinesen's writing, which is bound to come and which might fittingly be encouraged by the setting up of a Karen Blixen Society with the purpose, among others, of publishing dissertations on her works and memoirs of the character behind the works. Indeed there are many aspects to be explored.

The time has also come to approach the reality behind the myth in another way, by collecting and publishing the best of the photos connected with the name Isak Dinesen. Several have undoubtedly been destroyed by age, and Karen Blixen herself during her life in Africa attached no importance to preserving the visible world on the photographic plate, probably because she expected to spend her last days in Kenya. It is therefore rather fortuitous that what has been preserved from these eighteen important years is plentiful and the choice difficult. What exactly does one wish to tell by means of these pictures—what is the purpose of the book? Several, quite different, pictorial books could be made of Karen Blixen. No other Danish writer, not even Hans Christian Andersen, has been photographed as often as she. From the last fifteen years of her life alone, there exists such a tremendous amount of photographs, professional as well as amateur, that one could make a large, glamorous and fashionable pictorial work, telling the story of the lionized author as the center of a group of cosmopolitan artists and writers. Such a book would give an impression of the outgoing, vividly giving and receiving side of Karen Blixen's personality, but the portrait would lack perspective and depth because she was also a hard-working, contemplative and only seldom satisfied artist.

It has been the goal of this book to present two parallel traits in Karen Blixen's nature: her need for a first-hand experience of life—for being in the center of the action or being herself the action's center—and her drive to preserve the dying day, to create a spiritual world which was exclusively her own. She had several artistic talents; she tried her hand as a painter, acted in many of the situations of life with the true talent of an actress, but she was first and foremost a born writer and poet and during her youth bravely tried to follow her predestined calling in spite of various inner difficulties and the well-meaning indifference of her surroundings. She was to undergo nearly inhuman sorrows before the secret reserves of her soul broke through and conquered her inhibitions. Among the papers she left behind, there was a poem on the theme of sorrow, with which she was to become only too well acquainted, written before her twentieth year. The following is a free rendering of a few lines:

> O sacred sorrow, mother of all joy—
> Yearning to happiness, night to morning yields.
> The roads from unfulfilment to the light
> lead all across the land in which you reign.
> Light comes from darkness, daybreak comes from night
> through your purification, in your hands.
> All life you, sorrow, mother of our joy,
> lead to fulfilment where all changes end.

Despite its lack of originality this poem gives a strange glimpse of the inner life of the young Karen Blixen. What was awaiting her in Africa and later upon her return to Denmark was to partly affirm her youthful impression of life as a tragic affair. But the sensitiveness and seriousness of her nature was so much tempered by a great sense of humor and love of life, that at the end of the road she was able to think of her life as having been completely happy. It is a reflection of this rich play of light and shade in her nature that this book has tried to catch.

Clara Svendsen once said that at Rungstedlund, each night before she retired Karen Blixen opened the door to the yard and paused for a moment, then she went to "Ewald's Room," closing the door after her. After having witnessed this ceremony for fourteen years Clara Svendsen one day asked Karen Blixen what it meant. She explained that she opened the door to look towards Africa, and she went into Ewald's room to look at the map of her farm in the Ngong Hills. She did not mention a photograph that was standing on the window-sill by her desk, but there in fact was a portrait of Denys Finch-Hatton, her English friend, who was killed on the eve of her leaving Africa.

This tells a lot about Karen Blixen, about the longing for wings which penetrates all her life and writings. About her faithfulness to that which no longer existed in reality but only lived on in her mind. And of the irreparable losses of her life, the unhealed wounds, which enabled the artist in her to incorporate the experience of suffering into her work.

My wish is that this book, along with her own works, contributes to keeping the doors to the world of Karen Blixen open, a world unlike any other. The photographs can show us what it looked like to the ordinary eye, but they can never replace the mirror in which she saw it reflected. This was the secret of her genius, and that is beyond exploration.

Frans Lasson 15

Karen Blixen's great-grandfather Jens Kraft Dinesen (1768–1827); from 1801 owner of Kragerupgaard on central Zealand. Married to Ulrica Gøring.

Katholm Castle in Jutland, in the possession of the Dinesen family from 1839 to 1917, Karen Blixen's father's home as a child. It was acquired by her grandfather Adolph Wilhelm Dinesen, and inherited in 1876 by his eldest son, Laurentzius. Wentzel, Laurentzius Dinesen's son, died before his father, and at the death of Laurentzius, in 1916, there were two possible successors. His daughter, Agnes, would have first claim to Katholm if she agreed to retain and run the estate. However, since she did not wish to assume this obligation, the same offer was made to his nephew Thomas Dinesen, Karen Blixen's brother, but the best financial advisers that could be procured advised him strongly against accepting. Consequently, the estate passed to Agnes (married to Count Gebhard Knuth), who sold it. The fact that the family had had to give up Katholm never ceased to grieve Karen Blixen, and her memories of the place and all it had meant to her are reflected in the description she has given of it under the name of Ballegaard in "Copenhagen Season," in *Last Tales*.

Karen Blixen's paternal grandfather, Adolph Wilhelm Dinesen (1807–1876); officer and owner of Katholm Castle from 1839.

A. W. Dinesen was born at Kragerupgaard. In 1833, the year when he became a first lieutenant, he traveled with Hans Christian Andersen in Italy, from Milan to Rome, and they went on Roman excursions together. At Dinesen's departure, Andersen made this entry in his diary: "How very much I have learned from this young, determined person, who has so often hurt me in my affection for him.—If only I had his character, even with its flaws! Good-bye, D!—"

A. W. Dinesen was in command of a battery in the 1848–50 war against Prussia and Austria, fought in Schleswig. The first cannon shots of the war, on April 9 at Bov (a battle celebrated in one of the popular songs of the time) as well as the last ones, on December 31, 1850, were fired by the "Battery Dinesen."

He ran the Katholm estate diligently and with competence. Drawing by Niels Simonson, 1850.

Karen Blixen's great-grandfather, Lieutenant General Johan Wolfgang Reinholdt Haffner, of Egholm (1770–1829). After a portrait in the drawing room at Rungstedlund.

19

Jens Kraft Dinesen

married to Ulrica Gøring

A. W. Dinesen, owner of Katholm

Laurentzius Dinesen, owner of Katholm

Captain Wilhelm Dinesen ("Boganis"), Rungstedlund

General Joh. Wolfgang Reinholdt Haffner

Dagmar Alvilda Haffner

married to Anna Margrethe Kabøll

Six sisters

Anders Dinesen, Leerbæk

Karen Westenholz, married to Georg Sass, owner of Leerbæk

Thomas Dinesen, V.C married to Jonna Lindhardt

A. N. Hansen

married to Emma Eliza Grut

Mary Lucinde Hansen

Torben Westenholz

Ellen Dinesen, married to Knud Dahl, owner of Sandbjerg

Aage Westenholz

Karen Christentze Dinesen, married to Baron Bror von Blixen-Finecke

Thomas Frederik Westenholz, Skagen,

Regnar Westenholz, owner of Matrup

married to Anne Marie Elisabeth Aabel

Mary Bess Westenholz

Inger ("Ea") Dinesen, married to Viggo de Neergaard

Ingeborg Westenholz

KAREN BLIXEN'S PATERNAL AND MATERNAL FAMILY

Asker Westenholz

Hans Christian Andersen at Frijsenborg, with Count Frijs's three daughters and a cousin. On August 8, 1874, he wrote in a letter to Henriette Collin: "From Countess Frijs I received a letter yesterday, she informed me that her nephew Dinesen, who was a captain in the French Army, has for several years lived the life of a complete hermit in the American forests, and subsists on hunting, far from everyone. In his latest letter to her he tells her that on an excursion into the interior he came upon a lonely house, where he found one book. It was *Andersen's Fairy Tales*."

Agnes Krag-Juel-Vind-Frijs (1852–1871), daughter of Count Krag-
Juel-Vind-Frijs. She is the model for Adelaide in "Copenhagen Season":
"'The Rose of Jutland' they called her, as if all the land of the penin-
sula, from the dunes of the Skague to the pastures of Friesland, had
gone to make up soil for this one fragrant, fragile flower. . . . The
finest objects of the earth . . . had been hers all her life, by right of
birth and because it was felt that nothing else would go harmoniously
with the bright, frank figure." Grief over her untimely death—in Italy
of a sudden illness at the age of eighteen—contributed to the depres-
sion which drove Karen Blixen's father, Wilhelm Dinesen, out into the
wilds of America for two years.

The two sisters Thyra Valborg Haffner (1821–1881), married to Count Christian Emil Krag-Juel-Vind-Frijs, of Frijsenborg, for a time Prime Minister of Denmark, and Dagmar Alvilda Haffner (1818–1874), married to A. W. Dinesen, of Katholm.

Frijsenborg Castle in Jutland, the manor house of Denmark's largest estate, underwent radical reconstruction in the 1860's. Life here was resplendent, with big hunts and parties where crowned heads were among the guests. When entering upon her adult life, Karen Dinesen felt irresistibly drawn toward this place.

GEORG E. HANSEN PHOT.

Dinesen 1867

Of one of the characters in "Copenhagen Season" it is said: ". . . when young Princess Dagmar traveled to Russia to marry the Czarevitch Alexander, the eldest Angel brother, who was an officer in the guards, had been sent to escort her. Such a nomination against rules and reasonableness—since the young man possessed neither name, rank nor fortune—would have to be put down to his good looks, as if the Danish nation, after having delivered an exquisite specimen of its womanhood, wanted to display before its mighty neighbor and ally a fine sample of its young manhood."

Here is the model: Wentzel Laurentzius Dinesen (1843–1916), eldest son of A. W. Dinesen.

". . . the two young men were such close friends that the wits of their circle had given them but one name in common, creating a mythical figure which combined elegance and knowledge of the world with wild, wayward talents," it is said of two other characters in "Copenhagen Season." The models: the two cousins Mogens Krag-Juel-Vind-Frijs (1849–1923) and Wilhelm Dinesen (1845–1895).

The sisters Clara and Agnes Krag-Juel-Vind-Frijs at Frijsenborg in the 1860's.
In 1873 Clara married Baron Frederik Blixen-Finecke, of Näsbyholm in Skåne,
in southern Sweden, and in 1914 she became Karen Blixen's mother-in-law. 25

Eighteen-year-old Lieutenant Wilhelm Dinesen took part in the Dano-Prussian War of 1864. He was in the battles of Sankelmark and Dybbøl. His war experiences are described in a small book entitled *From the Eighth Brigade* (reprinted in 1945). Karen Blixen read from it over the Danish radio on her father's centennial, December 19, 1945, her first performance in a medium she was later to become very familiar with. The picture, showing Wilhelm Dinesen on the left with fellow officers Steinmann and Thestrup, was taken somewhere in the Dano-German borderland of Schleswig. Denmark lost the war, and grief over the defeat was an incentive for Wilhelm Dinesen's participation in the Franco-Prussian War six years later.

After serving as a captain in the French army in the war of 1870–71, Wilhelm Dinesen received the cross of the Legion of Honor, and Karen Blixen remembered that at his funeral there was a large wreath inscribed *"A un ami de la France."* But here he was to experience another defeat. The time he spent in Paris after the war, described in his book *Paris under the Commune*, was likewise rough fare, and to this was added the stunning blow of Agnes Frijs's untimely death. "Sick at heart" (he wrote later) he left for America. He spent a couple of years in the Middle West, most of the time living under primitive conditions as a trapper, and as a hermit as well, except for his association with the Chippewa Indians. He remained restless after his return to Denmark, and during the Russo-Turkish War he spent some time in Constantinople and the Balkans in 1877. Here again he was on the side of the loser.

Rungstedlund, about 1880.—In 1879 Wilhelm Dinesen, together with his sister Alvilda, bought Rungstedlund and Rungstedgaard in Rungsted, halfway between Copenhagen and Elsinore; the small property Sømandshvile (Sailor's Rest) half a mile south of Rungsted, and Folehavegaard near Hørsholm. The three properties comprised practically all the farm land between Rungsted on the sea and Hørsholm two miles inland. Wilhelm Dinesen, who was engaged to be married to Ingeborg Westenholz, moved into Rungstedlund, and the plan was that after the wedding they would move into the elegant mansion at Folehavegaard. However, he had grown so fond of Rungstedlund (previously Rungsted Inn) that he persuaded his fiancée to make their home there instead—"it was really almost asking too much of Mother," said Karen Blixen. The buildings were primitive and raised at random but, situated right by the sea and forming an organic relationship with the fishermen's cottages nearby, they presented a milieu of great charm. Moreover, this former inn, licensed about 1520, was of historic interest.

Karen Blixen's maternal grandfather, Regnar Westenholz (1815–1866). —After the death of his father, who had held the office of bailiff at Skagen, he became a merchant's apprentice at an early age, first in a nearby town and later in Hamborg, where, according to Karen Blixen, his sleeping quarters were under the counter. With exceptional drive and competence, he built up a large business of his own, and for a time had his main office and private residence in London. Later he acquired the estate of Matrup near Horsens in Jutland, which he ran as a model farm. He was Minister of Finance in the short-lived Rotwitt administration. Ever since his early youth he was a bibliophile; his collection of nineteenth-century Danish literature found its way to Rungstedlund with his daughter Ingeborg, and his granddaughter Karen Blixen brought the books with her to the African farm.

Matrup, Karen Blixen's mother's home as a child, seen from the mill pond. Photograph from the 1870's.

Karen Blixen's maternal grandmother, Mary Westenholz (1834–1915), whom children and grandchildren called "Mama." Here she poses with her sons, Asker, Aage and Torben; Regnar Westenholz's son by his first marriage, Thomas; and her daughters, Mary Bess, Ingeborg and Karen ("Aunt Lidda").

N.E.SINDING   PHOTOGRAPH.

Östergade 58. KJÖBENHAVN. (Kong Salomons Apothek.)

Etatsraad A. N. Hansen

Karen Blixen's great-grandfather, Andreas Nicolaj Hansen (1798–1873), one of the leading merchants of the time. He owned a town house in Bredgade, and it was probably his summer residence Øregaard in Hellerup that Karen Blixen had in mind when at the end of "The Pearls," in *Winter's Tales*, she mentions "her father's villa." The underlying motive in this short story is in fact the contrast which Karen Blixen felt between her maternal and paternal relatives. —A. N. Hansen was married to Emma Eliza Grut, who came from Guernsey. Of his numerous descendants, some have adopted the name Grut.

On May 17, 1881, Wilhelm Dinesen and Ingeborg Westenholz (born May 5, 1856, at Matrup) were married in Tyrsting Church. Her parents were Regnar Westenholz and Mary Lucinde Hansen, daughter of A. N. Hansen.

Wilhelm and Ingeborg Dinesen on the veranda at Rungstedlund, about 1888, with their three daughters: Inger, called Ea; Karen, called Tanne (with fingers in her mouth); and Ellen, called Elle. Two sons, Thomas and Anders, were born later.

Presumably the pet name Tanne is the result of Karen's first, vain attempts at pronouncing her own name. For as long as she lived, she remained "Tanne" to the family. Wilhelm Dinesen, who had lived in France, had yet another version of it which Karen Blixen recalled late in life: one day when he was returning home by sea from a trip abroad, she ran on ahead of the family, who had gone to meet him at the jetty, and he stood up in the boat and called "Hello, Ta-Ta!" using the pet name she would have had in Paris. She had also found out, probably from her mother, that he had once said, "Ea and Elle will be able to look after themselves, but my heart aches for little Tanne."

The farmyard at Rungstedlund, September 5, 1891.—Rungstedlund was a traditional Danish farmstead, with the buildings set on the four sides of the yard. The property was run as a farm until 1898, when a fire destroyed the outbuildings. Many people lived there: a large family in the rooms upstairs, and a large staff which sat down to lively meals in the semibasement facing south. Tanne felt much drawn toward this downstairs world, partly because it meant a chance of having coffee instead of tea, which was served upstairs, partly because of the interesting talk. The scene in "Peter and Rosa," in *Winter's Tales*, which begins, "She . . . decided that she would go down to the kitchen, to have her breakfast," is straight out of life at Rungstedlund, including the fisherwoman's name, Emma.

Karen Dinesen, two or three years old. In the chair, her elder sister, Ea.

Tanne, Elle and Ea (born April 17, 1885; September 13, 1886; and April 2, 1883, respectively).

Christentze Dinesen (1854–1920), the youngest but one of Wilhelm Dinesen's six sisters and godmother of Karen Dinesen, whose middle name was Christentze, after her godmother. She was married to Christian Neergaard of Aakjær, and was the model for Drude in "Copenhagen Season."

In 1882 Count Mogens Krag-Juel-Vind-Frijs took over the northern part of the estate of Frijsenborg, and in 1884 he married Frederikke Danneskiold-Samsøe—"Aunt Fritze" to Karen Blixen. Of the five children born to Wilhelm Dinesen, Mogens' childhood friend, it was Tanne in particular who was enchanted by her father's friends.

Laurentzius Dinesen, of Katholm, the young lieutenant in the photograph on page 24, here photographed in the year 1900.—This was the time when "Uncle Laurentzius" had heated discussions with Karen Dinesen and the other youth of the family about whether it was proper for a lady to ride a bicycle, as described in her essays, *Daguerreotypes:* "He was a blusterer and a domestic tyrant, and a beautiful woman or a shrewd old servant could turn him round their little finger."

Wilhelm Dinesen with fellow sportsmen at Sannarp estate in Halland, Sweden. Far right: the host, Michael Treschow.

BOGANIS:

JAGTBREVE

MED VIGNETTER AF HANS NIK. HANSEN

KJØBENHAVN
P. G. PHILIPSENS FORLAG
THIELES BOGTRYKKERI
1889

Wilhelm Dinesen's literary work was not extensive but it shows unmistakable originality. *Jagtbreve* (Letters from the Hunt) (1889) and *Nye Jagtbreve* (New Letters from the Hunt) (1892), published under the pseudonym of Boganis, are discursive essays with hunting experiences as the basic theme, which are constantly being reprinted. His qualities as a writer were acknowledged by Georg Brandes, the most important Danish literary critic at the time. Wilhelm Dinesen himself, however, was reluctant to take writing seriously. The Norwegian dramatist and novelist Nordahl Grieg found some of the material for his play *The Defeat* (1937) in Dinesen's *Paris under the Commune.*

37

Ea, Thomas, Elle and Tanne.
November 1, 1893.

The three sisters with Thomas
in a baby carriage.

Ingeborg Dinesen with her
three daughters, Elle, Ea and
Tanne, and her son Thomas
(born August 9, 1892). The
photograph was probably taken
in the summer of 1893 at Folehave.

Ingeborg Dinesen with her children and their governess, Miss Zøylner.
—Karen Blixen remembered that her father had once announced his
intention to advertise for a governess who could drink half a bottle
of red wine a day, as there was no one with whom he could share a
bottle. It is doubtful, though, that Miss Zøylner fulfilled this require-
ment.—The girls' education was mostly their mother's and grandmother's department.

Various factors allegedly contributed to Wilhelm Dinesen's suicide,
on March 28, 1895; he ended his life by hanging himself in the board-
inghouse in Copenhagen where he used to stay when Parliament was
in session. One day shortly before his death Malla, the children's nanny
(who was to remain at Rungstedlund for the rest of her life), entered
his study in order to deliver a message; he did not hear or see her but
continued to pace the floor, mumbling, "I'll have to do it, I'll have to
do it." Karen Blixen believed that fear of an incurable illness, which
would make him a burden to his family, was behind his decision.

Thomas and Anders Dinesen at their father's grave in the Hørsholm Cemetery, March 1899.

May 27, 1896—Karen Dinesen, her sisters and her friends, performing a comedy, *Pride Goeth before a Fall*, by the eleven-year-old author. The picture was taken outside the veranda at Rungstedlund. The children staged many plays of their own invention. On one occasion they asked a member of the family to spare a moment to act the part of a bluish mist. —Only one of the comedies, *The Revenge of Truth*, survived from that time, to be rewritten later.

Like her mother, Ingeborg Dinesen found herself left with the responsibility for a family. Tanne had been extremely close to her father, and of the children, she was probably the one who suffered most at the time of his death. She was at Folehave with her maternal relatives when she received the tidings. The children had been told that he was ill. When one of the aunts came into the room Tanne asked, "How is Father?" and was told that he had died. After a while her sister Ea said to one of the grownups, "Tanne is trembling so." Among the many bleak memories of the time that followed there was also an admonition: "A widow's children must behave better than other children."

Folehave.—Ingeborg Dinesen's mother and eldest sister had moved over from Matrup and settled here. "Mama" and Aunt Bess gave Ingeborg Dinesen a great deal of support after Wilhelm Dinesen's death; the residents of Rungstedlund and Folehave paid one another daily visits; and on Sundays the whole family dined together at Folehave. Tanne had difficulty adapting herself to this life, to a large degree because she encountered the hostile attitude of her maternal relatives toward her father, his relatives and friends. But many years later, when she had come back from Africa and was again living at Rungstedlund, she was unsparing in her devoted attention to old Aunt Bess and sat at her deathbed. She had made a maxim of the words "I will not let thee go except thou bless me."

Ingeborg Dinesen with her five children, about 1896. Tanne is far left. The youngest, Anders, was born May 8, 1894. Thomas, who enlisted in the Canadian army during the First World War and was decorated with the Victoria Cross, is here seen holding his first gun.

44

Holiday at Kullen, on the Swedish coast, probably the year after Wilhelm Dinesen's death. In the center, Ingeborg Dinesen with the youngest child, Anders. Behind her is "Mama," her mother. Both maternal aunts are here too: in the background, Aunt Lidda, and in front, in a straw hat, Aunt Bess. Mary Bess Westenholz later became quite famous after an incident in Parliament, where she made her way from the gallery to the platform, rang the Chairman's bell and on behalf of Danish women delivered an indignant contribution to the debate.— The children on the left are Ea and Elle, on the right Thomas and Tanne. In the background is Malla, their beloved nanny.

Karen Blixen had been writing poetry ever since her childhood. Old notebooks seem to indicate that she and her sisters were instructed by Aunt Bess in the art of writing verse. There are model poems in Aunt Bess's handwriting on the left-hand page, and the children's attempts on the right. The unpublished poem reproduced here was probably written between the ages of fifteen and twenty.

Tanne dressed up as "Mama," about 1900.

Rosenholm, 400-year-old manor of the Rosenkrantz family, friends of the Dinesens, whom Tanne visited when staying at Katholm.

At the age of fifteen, Karen Dinesen made ten drawings illustrating *A Midsummer Night's Dream* (one of them shown below) and even before that time she had sketched some of the characters in *As You Like It*. She also made sketches for Dickens' *A Tale of Two Cities*.

On the opposite page: Illustrations for one of Karen Dinesen's own unfinished stories, "A Tale of the French Revolution." From her early youth she was especially familiar with this particular period, which was also the setting of several of the later tales belonging to the mature period of her writing.

"Mama's" seventieth birthday, on July 25, 1904, at Munkebjerg in Jutland. Top row, left to right: Ellen Dinesen, George Sass (Aunt Lidda's husband), Ulla Westenholz, Aage Westenholz, Asker Westenholz, Karen Dinesen, the matron at Matrup, and Sanne, the old nanny. Center row: Ea Dinesen, Mary Bess Westenholz, "Mama," Ingeborg Dinesen and Karen Sass (Aunt Lidda). Bottom row: Thomas Westenholz, Elsebet Westenholz, Anders Dinesen and Thomas Dinesen.

Aunt Bess, imposingly erect and militant here as always, wrote a long and interesting (never printed) chronicle of "Mama" and life at Matrup. It is hard to believe that Aunt Lidda was not yet forty-five when this picture was taken. The eldest of the Westenholz sisters, Ingeborg, here nearly fifty and for nine years the widowed mother of five, seems the one who carried her age most gracefully. One of the words which Karen Blixen would later use to characterize her mother was indeed "graceful" and Wilhelm Dinesen's choice of a bride is easy to understand. Here, as in the picture from Kullen (page 45), a face radiating goodness and gentleness is seen in the background: in the Rungsted household Malla, at Matrup Sanne.

The three Dinesen sisters, about 1903.—Ea studied singing at the Royal Academy of Music and gave some concerts. In 1916 she married Viggo de Neergaard, of Valdemarskilde, but she died already in 1922, leaving a small daughter, Karen. Ellen shared the musical interest of Ea and the literary interest of Tanne; as a young girl she played the violin, and later wrote books which were published under the pseudonym of Paracelsus. She, too, married in 1916. Her husband, Knud Dahl, was a lawyer; they both took a heartfelt interest in the problems of the Dano-German borderland of Schleswig, and in 1930 acquired the Sandbjerg estate near Dybbøl, which after his death was donated to the University of Aarhus.

51

Karen Dinesen and her cousin Thomas Westenholz, of Matrup, here photographed at Leerbæk.

Leerbæk, near Vejle in Jutland.—Karen Westenholz, Ingeborg Dinesen's youngest sister, married the owner of Leerbæk, Georg Sass. Karen Blixen's reminiscences of "Aunt Lidda," "Uncle Gex" and life at Leerbæk could fill several pages, and still more might have been written by Anders Dinesen, who inherited Leerbæk after he had lived there for many years, in the separate smaller house called "Hopballehus"—the name Karen Blixen used for one of the characters in "The Monkey," in *Seven Gothic Tales*. At present the estate is owned by Hans Dinesen, Thomas Dinesen's younger son.

Whenever Karen Blixen mentioned "Glenstriven," to her it conjured up summer holidays and happy family visits. It was the summer residence of her Scottish relatives, the Berrys. "Mama's" elder sister, Emily, had married Walter Berry, the consul general for Denmark in Edinburgh. All of Karen Blixen's lifetime connections were kept up with this branch of the numerous clan, the descendants of A. N. Hansen.

The student glee club visiting Rungstedlund on Midsummer Day 1905. Front row: Ea, Tanne, Ingeborg Dinesen and Elle.

Karen and Thomas Dinesen, July 19, 1907.—The following is a quotation from Thomas Dinesen's contribution to *Isak Dinesen: A Memorial*, published in 1965: "How proud I was when the time came that my sister started to talk with me as if I were an equal—she about twenty years of age and I only twelve or thirteen!" In this photograph she is twenty-two, Thomas nearly sixteen. He continued: ". . . how desperately she longed for wings to carry her away . . ."—and one realizes that it was difficult for her to endure this kind of quiet existence until she was twenty-eight. In her old age she said, "I really don't understand how we managed to pass the time." The close friendship with her brother which was established during these years meant much to her in later, difficult times, in Africa and after her return to Denmark.

Karen Dinesen with Thomas' first boat, *Basia*, named after the heroine in the novel *Pan Wolodjowsky*, by Henryk Sienkiewicz.—Sailing with her brothers, Thomas and Anders, is reflected in some of her early poems, such as "Fair Wind" (published in *Osceola*, 1962), and "Rowing Song," which is reminiscent of Boganis: the light boat swept along by the currents is seen as an image of the irresolute mind set adrift by "imagination and fantasy, old tales and thoughts at twilight, words and moods and dreams."

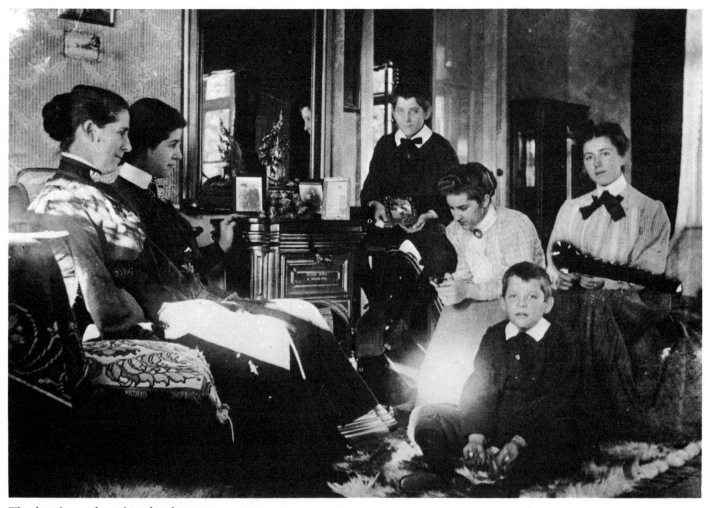

The family, gathered in the drawing room at Rungstedlund, about 1904. From left to right: Mrs. Ingeborg Dinesen, Elle, Thomas, Ea, Anders and Tanne.

Karen Dinesen and a friend on board the *Basia* with Thomas and Anders, October 3, 1906.—Some years later they had a bigger boat, with sails. During a storm the *Wing* took in so much water that it quietly sank at its moorings; no one was hurt, but a friend of the family who witnessed the incident telephoned and said, "We stood there and saw it happen . . . how terrible . . . the only comfort is, it's really nothing compared to the *Titanic*."

Opposite page: Karen Dinesen, sketching at Kullen, July 15, 1907. By this time she had acquired professional training at the Royal Academy of Fine Arts. The charcoal drawings on the next two pages are works from her student days.

Charlottenborg Castle, home of the Royal Academy of Fine Arts in Copenhagen. —Karen Dinesen assiduously entered upon one of the few regular fields of education open to women at the turn of the century: from 1902 to 1903 she took drawing lessons at the private art school of the Misses Sode and Meldahl to qualify for admission to the academy. The drawing she submitted with her entrance application was approved and she was admitted in 1903; her teacher was Professor Viggo Johansen. In Paris in 1910, lacking contact with the circles where art was really alive, she made a half-hearted attempt to continue her studies; the art school she had chosen, the Académie de Simon et Ménard, made scant impression on her. Later she took lessons from the Danish painter Bertha Dorph.

Late in life Karen Blixen said of herself and the best friends of her youth, "We were dying to have a good time." This photograph was taken around 1907, when "The Hermits" and "The Ploughman" were published. Some accounts from that period are still extant. There is an entry for an evening gown on the debit side, while on the credit side there are figures representing regular pocket money and the author's fee for "The Ploughman." Unless the latter was an installment, the cost of the evening gown exceeded the author's fee. But she looks very pleased with her finery.

KCDinnesen

MARIA GRAZIE GIACONELLI

Mario Krohn (1881–1922), an art historian, later director of the Thorvaldsen Museum, and one of the intellectuals among Karen Dinesen's friends, was the first to guide her along the road to a literary career. He put her in touch with *Tilskueren* magazine (The Spectator), read the proofs of "The Hermits," and after he became the editor of the magazine, published "The de Cats Family." She often met him in Paris while she and her sister Ea were staying there, from March 25 to June 1, 1910.

Dr. Valdemar Vedel (1865–1942) was a literary historian and the editor of *Tilskueren* (The Spectator) at the time when Karen Dinesen was encouraged by Mario Krohn to send in "The Hermits." His reply of October 17, 1906, to the author (opposite page) indicates that a second manuscript had been submitted at the same time and that this was found unsuitable. Apparently the length of "The Hermits" caused him some misgivings, but he found it so extraordinary and in many ways so well done that he was prepared to print it if it were cut somewhat. The letter concludes: "No doubt the author has talent."

TILSKUERENS
REDAKTION

DR. VALD. VEDEL
NØJSOMHEDSV. 17
Tlf. Ø 958 y

$\frac{17}{10}$ 1906.

Kære Fröken!

Vedlagt sender jeg Dem begge Manuskripter tilbage; det har desværre taget nogen Tid, inden jeg fik dem rigtig ordentlig læst og fik taget min Bestemmelse. Deres Snedag har interesseret mig, og jeg synes, det er udmærket formet og stemt til Brug for jævn menneskelig Opbyggelse. Men jeg tror ikke, at vil "gøre sig" som Afhandling i et Tidsskrift, dertil er vaad hele Samlesbemmen for bred og lidt kunstnerisk udarbejdet og hele Tonen for enfoldig-hjertelig (om jeg saa maa sige); under Tidsskriftlæsning er man nu en Gang saa at sige indstillet paa en mere praktisk ræsonnementsmæssig Udvikling. Det er dernæst altfor langt, til at jeg turde binde an med det. Længere er ogsaa det, der giver mig Betænkeligheder m. H. t. Fortællingen om "Emborgne". Den er ellers saa ejendommelig og paa mange Punkter saa godt gjort, at jeg gerne vilde tage den til "Tilskueren", hvor man trænger til den Slags Fantasiunderholdning. Og hvis det — hvad Indfatterinden alene kan bedømme — skulde være lettrist at faa den forkortet med c. 10 Sider (dernæst maatte jo forlængst uspildferdi Ord og Sætninger rundt om i Manuskriptet udfyldes), vilde den godt kunne Optages i Tidsskriftet. Sammen med et Par andre lignende Sandsynlige "Historier" vilde den ogsaa virkelig med Deres kunne udkomme som Bog. De er sikkert Talent i Infatterinden.

Deres ærbødige Vald. Vedel.

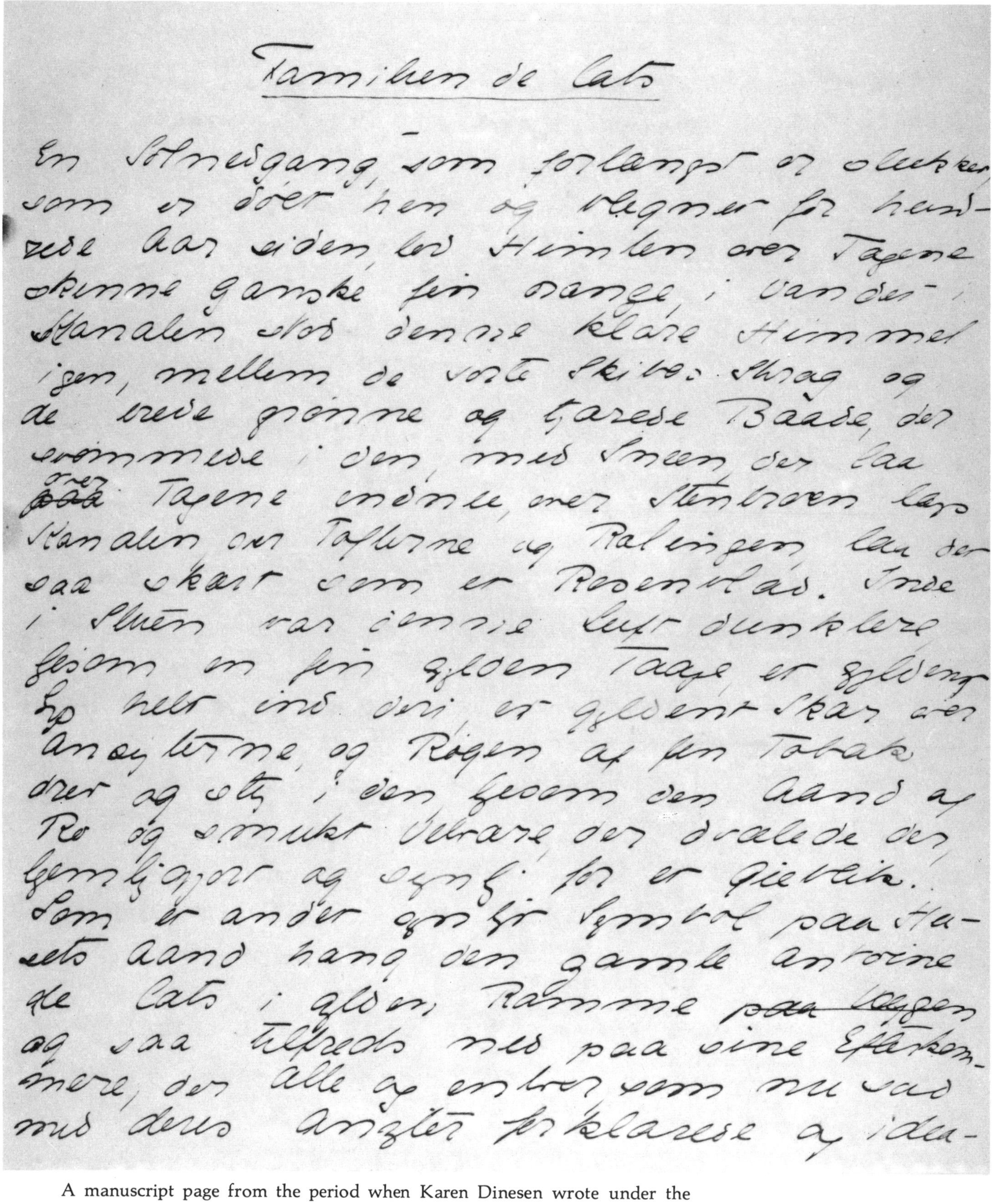
Familien de Cats

En Solnedgang, som forlængst er slukket, som er død hen og blegner for hundrede Aar siden, lod Himlen over Tagene skinne ganske fin orange, i Vander-Kanalen stod denne klare Himmel igen, mellem de sorte Skibes Skrog og de brede grønne og tjærede Baade, der svømmede i den, med Sneen, der laa ~~paa~~ over Tagene endnu, over Stenbroen langs Kanalen over Toflerne og Rælingen laa der saa skært som et Rosenblad. Inde i Stuen var imidlertid luft dunklere gjennem en fin gylden Taage, et gyldent lys helt ind deri, et gyldent Skær over Ansigterne, og Røgen af fin Tobak drev og steg i den gjennem den Aand af Ro og smukt Velvære der dvælede der hemmelighedsfuldt og synligt for et Øjeblik. Som et andet og fint Symbol paa Husets Aand hang den gamle Antoine de Cats i gylden Ramme ~~paa Væggen~~ og saa tilfreds ned paa sine Efterkommere, der alle og enhver som nu sad med deres Ansigter forklarede af idea-

A manuscript page from the period when Karen Dinesen wrote under the pseudonym of Osceola: the opening lines of "The de Cats Family." They were not used in the final version, which was printed in *Tilskueren* in 1909.

ENEBOERNE

ENNE Historie om Eneboerne begynder med et Brev:

Min øde Ø, 1779.

Mine kæreste Søstre.

Det skal være det allerførste, jeg gør, nu, da jeg har et Øjeblik tilovers, at skrive til jer. Jeg véd nok, at dette Brev ikke vil naa jer før om lang Tid, om Maaneder eller et halvt Aar maaske, men dog skriver jeg det, for jeg kan ikke holde ud, at I ikke skal vide lige saa god Besked og kende alt her lige saa godt som jeg. — Men jeg er endnu saa fortumlet af at gynge op og ned paa Vejen herover, — det er, som om mine Tanker endnu gyngede, — at I ikke maa vente, dette skal blive noget fornuftigt Brev. Der har ogsaa ramt os en stor Sorg. Den lille Dreng, som vi havde med os til Øen, Joseph, er død, han maa være falden ned fra en Klippe ved Stranden og druknet, det var to Dage efter at vi kom hertil, — saa er det syv Dage siden, i Dag. Det forekommer mig allerede at være uendelig længe siden. Det forfærdede mig og tog mit Mod fra mig, saaledes at det først var i Gaar Aftes, da jeg gjorde Ild paa og kom til at tænke paa, hvordan han gjorde Ilden op den første Aften, vi var her, at jeg kom til at græde over ham, og nu græder jeg, hver Gang jeg tænker paa ham, og hvor langt mere føler man ikke Savnet, naar man er saa alene. Han skulde have hjulpet mig med Husèt, og jeg tror ikke, det Arbejde vil være vanskeligt for mig alene, men hans arme Forældre, der saa ham drage af Sted saa glad! — Og er det ikke en forunderlig

The first page of "The Hermits" as printed in *Tilskueren*, August 1907, under the pseudonym of Osceola.

In "Copenhagen Season," Karen Blixen describes the town houses in Copenhagen belonging to the nobility and the part they played in the winter season of the city. Below: The town house owned by Count Krag-Juel-Vind-Frijs, of Frijsenborg, on the corner of the Frederiksholms Kanal and the Ny Kongensgade. It still belongs to the family and is now the Wedell mansion. Left: the second generation of close friendships in the Frijs-Dinesen families—Daisy and Tanne. Daisy, whose real name was Anne Margrethe, was the daughter of Count Mogens Frijs, and the best friend Tanne ever had. She was an exceptionally elegant and charming young woman but she did not find much personal happiness in life. She died in 1917, only twenty-nine years old.

At the horse races at Klampenborg, just outside Copenhagen.—Tanne, exuberant and ready to savor all that life had to offer, loved to go to the races and desperately wanted to wear elegant clothes that were just right for these occasions in spite of Aunt Bess's disapproval of such activities. It was a great moment in the racing world when Hans von Blixen-Finecke from Näsbyholm, of the Frijsenborg and Skåne set, on one and the same day won a race at Klampenborg, flew his own plane across the Sound to Malmö, and won there too.—Many years later Karen Blixen summed up this period of her life in these words: "More than anything, a deep, unrequited love left its mark on my early youth."

An inherited friendship: Else Bardenfleth and Karen Dinesen, whose mothers Ida Bardenfleth and Ingeborg Dinesen were friends.—In 1910 Else Bardenfleth (1884–1964) married Count Eduard Reventlow (1883–1963), who was the Danish ambassador in London during the Second World War. The Dinesen sisters maintained a lifelong contact with their girl friends from the Rungstedlund days. Until her dying day Countess Else Reventlow knew by heart long passages of Karen Dinesen's comedies and other early works written for domestic consumption.

Opposite page: Karen Dinesen, photographed just before she left for Africa.—In 1913 she had become engaged to Baron Bror von Blixen-Finecke (1886–1946), twin brother of Hans. They had decided to emigrate, and her fiancé left for British East Africa to buy land for the coffee plantation they wanted to start. When she was gone, Malla remarked back at Rungstedlund, "Now Mrs. Dinesen has lost the last of the Captain." Along with another memorable comment, by a relative —"Mutt [i.e., Tanne's mother, Ingeborg Dinesen] was taken by storm" —it shows that the description of Malli and her mother in "Tempests," in *Anecdotes of Destiny*, reflects the situation of young, impatient Karen Dinesen and her mother.

General Paul von Lettow-Vorbeck (1870–1964) went to German East Africa on the same ship which took Karen Dinesen to Mombasa in December 1913 – January 1914. They became friends, and this caused her a good deal of trouble when the war broke out and she was suspected by this British colony of sympathizing with the Germans. The general became renowned as a brilliant strategist and a gallant enemy, and she wrote later that the English "came to feel a sort of fondness for him . . . the same kind of fondness the hunter feels for an especially fine quarry." In 1940 Karen Blixen visited him in Bremen, and in 1958 in Hamburg accompanied by Thomas Dinesen, who had fought on the opposite side in the war.

Opposite page: The first entry in Bror Blixen's illustrated safari diary, which he sent home to his parents in Skåne in 1914: "After one week of target practice at home on M'bagathi we started out . . ." In a letter to her mother, Karen Blixen told about the same safari: "Bror has taught me how to handle a gun and says that I shoot well." Below: Karen and Bror Blixen with a bag of two lions.

Efter en veckas skjutöfningar hemma på Mbegathi startade vi den 5:te på morgonen från Kijabe. Redan klockan 5 kom Faras väckte oss kopp varm och med en kaffe. Det blef snart liv i lägret Mulorna derför till rattning vagnarne lastades och ruuades och vid 8 tiden kunde den första vagnen tänna — tungt lastad och förspänd med 8 mulor. Då kom en half timma senare N:o 2 med 4 mulor samt sist Faran och jag i en bekväm Amerikansk vagn dragen af ett par nätta mulor. Vi eskorterades af 1 somali (Fara) till häst. Kocken Esman på mule visade sig äfven trots sina sextio år som en uthållig ryttare.

Vägen var först dålig. Den gångna regnperiodens påminnelse hade skurit djupa fåror öfver vägen men väl uue på Kedong dalens slätter blef det godt före och i rask traf kunde vi tillryggelägga de Tjugo milen till vår första lägerplats vid foten af mount Souswa.

Klockan var nu två och den sena lunchen smakade förträffligt. Före oss var här en stor safari i läger

Karen Blixen outside the safari tent, 1914.

Karen and Bror Blixen's first farm was called M'bagathi, the purchase of which was financed by Karen Blixen's mother and by her uncle Aage Westenholz. Later on they acquired a much bigger farm, financed by both families as a shareholding company.

Opposite page, bottom: Bror Blixen outside the house, with three Swedish assistants. Left: The floor plan was sent home to Mrs. Ingeborg Dinesen. This first house was only a small bungalow; the veranda, shown in the photograph below, was added after the house was bought.

The living room at M'bagathi House, in the main building. This photograph was found in an album where it was the only one still fairly well preserved. The small French clock, a wedding present, followed Karen Blixen when she returned to Denmark, and can be seen in the photograph of her bedroom facing the Sound (page 220).

72   Bror Blixen inspecting a coffee field, 1914.

After the first year of marriage, Karen Blixen had to go home to Denmark
to be treated for a venereal disease which she had contracted through no fault
of her own. Too much time had elapsed before she set out; the journey took
very long because of war conditions; and when she arrived in Denmark it
took time to make discreet arrangements, which Karen Blixen insisted on,
in order to keep her mother, with her Puritan upbringing, in ignorance of the
situation. Karen Blixen herself believed that the long, hard years of illness
she had to endure later in life were a result of this disease. It was with open
eyes that she entered upon the same fate which she thought had threatened
her father.

Above: Crossing a river; photograph from Bror Blixen's safari diary. Below, right: Domestic idyll in a *manyatta*.

Opposite page: Karen Blixen and her mother in the yard at Rungstedlund during her visit to Denmark in 1915.

Sixteen years later, when Karen Blixen had to leave Africa for good and came back to live with her mother, she did not go riding any more. The contrast between northern Zealand and the vast plains of Africa was too great. But in the stable at Rungstedlund the stalls carrying the names of the horses can still be seen.

Oxen outside one of the farmhouses.

Africans who have come to look for work on the farm.

The warlike Masai, whose territory bordered on the property, attracted Karen Blixen's interest from the very start, as can be seen in the letters she sent home. She wrote that almost every day she went riding in the Masai Reserve and often tried to talk with the tall, handsome natives, and that they were always friendly and looked you straight in the face. In the poem "Ex Africa," which Karen Blixen wrote during her forced stay in Denmark in 1915, the phrase "in Masai Reserve" is constantly recurring. In the years after the Second World War she would talk about the acts of injustice and cruelty committed toward the native Africans which were unsurpassed by anything that had happened to other people in the world, and she mentioned with special indignation the plight of the Masai. They were deprived of their land and forced to move away, and later on their new land was taken away from them and once again they were moved elsewhere.

The residence at the new and bigger farm, situated in a place which was called M'bogani by the natives; the two farms were run concurrently. — The double consonants *mb* and *ng* were usually simplified to *b* and *g* in the English pronunciation of place names, and in a photograph from the early years the name "Bogani House" appears — almost the same as "Boganis," the name the American Indians had given Karen Blixen's father, and she may have taken this to be a good omen.

The farm at the foot of the Ngong Hills was one of the largest planta-
tions in Kenya. They usually comprised 100–150 acres of cultivated
land, but Karen Coffee had 600 acres of coffee and 200 acres of corn.
The main house, which served as living quarters and office to a farmer
in charge of 6,000 acres, might be considered of modest dimensions.
Karen Blixen describes how she used to sit in the evening with her
accounts and estimates spread over the dinner table. But in a moment
of crisis, one of her Danish relatives and shareholders who had come
out to evaluate the advisability of further investments wanted Karen
Blixen, as a token of good faith, to move into a small house of the most
primitive kind.—To save the farm would probably have taken the
genius of a Regnar Westenholz to come up with something entirely
new. If it could have been saved, there would have been one great book
less in the world. But it is probably safe to say that Karen Blixen did
not exaggerate when she claimed that had she remained on the farm she
might have contributed to a harmonious political development, especially in regard to the interracial situation.

Interior of the spacious new house described in *Out of Africa*. *Above:* Bror
and Karen Blixen in the drawing room. Opposite page: Karen Blixen at her
desk; Karen Blixen's bedroom.

The dining room.—Here company sat down to a table decked with silver, crystal and flowers and with Kamante's culinary artistry, and were waited upon by Farah the major-domo and Juma the servant. The guests were not only friends who came regularly but there were occasional visitors as well, from the Prince of Wales to "Emmanuelson" the fugitive.—There were, however, long periods of loneliness in between. Then the dining room was put to other uses. Like so many other authors, Karen Blixen would settle down at the dinner table when she wanted to do some serious writing. Her servants were hoping that her labor at the typewriter might help save the farm, and all through the evening they would stand stock-still against the wall, watching her. Since their dark faces were hardly visible against the dark wood paneling, it looked as if long white gowns were keeping her company. This is where she told Kamante about Odysseus, and Farah about Shylock and *The Merchant of Venice*.

Karen Blixen with eight Africans in front of the house. — Like the interior shots, this picture is from an album sent home to the family to show the new house. Second from left in the front row is Farah, who had been hired by Bror Blixen in 1913 and was sent to Aden to meet Tanne Dinesen and accompany her on the last leg of the voyage to Mombasa. In her very first letters home she wrote of Farah's good qualities. — The long necklace of big amber beads which she wears in this and several other pictures was a gift from Farah.

Opposite page: Thomas Dinesen during the First World War.*—After graduating from the Polytechnic Institute in 1916, Thomas Dinesen wanted to take an active part in the war—a natural outlet for his urge to try his mettle. Unable to get to France or England direct, he managed to get to Canada via the United States. He was accepted by the Royal Highlanders of Canada, the Black Watch. After basic military training he arrived in France in March 1918 and was in active service on the Lens-Amiens front until September. He received the Victoria Cross for extraordinary valor, as well as the French Croix de Guerre. As a veteran he was offered an opportunity to acquire land in Kenya and considered settling there. He spent several months during 1921–23 and 1924–25 with the Karen Coffee Company. His presence was a help and support to his sister. Heavy economic problems, illness and loneliness frequently plunged her into deep despondency. In 1921 she and Bror Blixen had separated, and the last ten years she managed the farm alone. At that point several of her relatives in Denmark had again contributed capital to the venture.

The house seen from another angle. In front, Karen Blixen with one of her dogs.

Cows by the dam.—"Old Knudsen," a Dane whose real name was
Aarup and who had knocked about a good deal, came to the farm
"sick and blind, and stayed there for the time it took him to die, a
lonely animal." He was always busy thinking up grandiose schemes.
One of his more realistic projects was the building of a dam, to provide
the farm with an artificial lake for the cattle. By primitive means and
with much difficulty the dam was built. It became an important element
in the life of the farm, always alive with children and animals along
the banks, and in the dry season a refuge for many kinds of birds.

Karen Blixen outside Old Knudsen's house. — His most ambitious venture was the exploitation of the hundred thousand tons of guano which since the creation of the world must have sunk to the bottom of Lake Naivasha from the birds living by the lake; it would make him a millionaire and put all his enemies to shame. He had no chance whatever of realizing the project, but three decades later Karen Blixen received a letter informing her that technical experts were now planning extraction of chemicals from Lake Naivasha. Old Knudsen had been proved right, after all. — When he died he left Karen Blixen a legacy of trouble with the authorities. Among other things, she was suspected of having murdered him.

To have one or more dogs remained at all times a natural thing to Karen Blixen, who was country-bred. In Africa she owned a family of Scotch deerhounds, beginning with Dusk and Dawn, a wedding present. Eighteen years later, when she had to return to Denmark, she left the two last ones, David and Dinah, with a friend near Gil-Gil, "where they would get good hunting." In the meantime, the breed was known in the colony as "the Lioness' dogs." It is said that an African gunbearer by mistake addressed a letter to "Lioness Blixen." The name stuck, and some years later, when her marriage had been dissolved and there was a new Baroness Blixen, she remained "the Lioness"—a title she held undisputed.

Karen Blixen feeding Lulu.—The chapter about Lulu is one of the best-known in the book about the farm. All through one long, hot day the tiny bushbuck was being offered for sale at the roadside by some African boys. Karen Blixen drove past them on her way out and saw them again in the evening when she returned home. A little later, after she had gone to bed, she suddenly realized she had acted "like the priest and the Levite in one," and moved heaven and earth to rescue the ill-treated little fawn. It became an inmate of the farm and was a great joy to Karen Blixen, her friends and staff.

Opposite page: Karen Blixen in riding habit, holding a rose; beside her stands Dusk. This is a snapshot taken somewhere on the farm in 1919, the year she met Denys Finch-Hatton.

Ingrid Lindström (left). "It was a joyful time when Ingrid came to stay with me," wrote Karen Blixen. She and her husband, Gillis Lindström, had come out from Sweden convinced that they would make a fortune quickly, but their particular speculation, in flax, failed completely. Ingrid then put in all her strength to save their farm, working like a slave, and succeeded. The description of her last visit, when Karen Blixen had lost her farm, is unforgettable.—Below: Ingrid Lindström's house at Njoro.

Farah Aden, a Somali of the Habr Yunis tribe. About the same age as Karen Blixen, he died during the Second World War. Her major-domo and personal attendant all the years in Africa, unswervingly loyal. When everything was lost and the end approaching, Farah brought out his most magnificent clothes and ornaments, and resplendent "like the Caliph Harun al-Rashid's own bodyguard" he followed her, erect and proud, on her supplicant expeditions up and down the streets of Nairobi. "No friend, brother or lover could have done for me what my servant Farah then did."

She reserved for oral comment the incident when a white man one day kicked Farah in the street of Nairobi, shouting, "Get off the side-walk, you damn nigger!"

this is photograph
of farah Adan &
his two Boys

10. 2. 33.

Nairobi

Farah with his son called Saufe, born in 1928, and Saufe's little brother. This photograph was sent to Karen Blixen in Denmark in 1933, two years after she left Africa but before her first book had appeared and made her famous as a writer. She started corresponding at once with the people she had left behind in Africa, and Farah was the central link in the connection.

Kikuyu girls dressed for a gala occasion. They are wearing the same type of headdress as the girl whose portrait Karen Blixen painted (see page 101).

One of the old women who supposedly took on the shape of hyenas at night.—The belief in witchcraft and sorcery could bring about complications and a nightmarish atmosphere, as was described in the chapter called "A Shooting Accident." Farah spoke of Kikuyu witchcraft with the same kind of concern that he would feel if they had had foot-and-mouth disease on the farm.

Old Kikuyus in front of the house. They look just like the old man who, after the *ngoma* (dancing) in honor of the Prince of Wales, made a formal little speech to say how pleased he and his companions had been to see "Memsahib" wearing a beautiful gown on that occasion, "for we all think that here, every day on the farm, you are terribly badly dressed."—Below: Nairobi in the 1920's, photographed by Thomas Dinesen.

Opposite page: Denys George Finch-Hatton (April 23, 1887–May 14, 1931), son of the Earl of Winchilsea and Nottingham.

When Karen Blixen grew up, she formed two completely different kinds of friendships: the intellectual friends she made at home and among her mother's family, and through her art studies and literary aspirations; then, there were the friends and relatives on the country estates, who preferred the out of doors and who were, with few exceptions, not intellectual at all. Her husband belonged to the latter category; he was a superb hunter and cattle breeder but would, as often as not, spell it "cattel."

Her best friends in Africa possessed the two kinds of qualities, particularly Denys Finch-Hatton, in whom a classical background from Eton and Oxford and a gift for music were combined with a splendid physique, keen senses and the practical ability which was indispensable for a first-class safari leader.

What he meant to her as a human being can be read between the lines of the pages she herself wrote about him. There is no doubt whatever that he must have influenced her development as a writer in a decisive way. To keep pace with him intellectually must have been no mean challenge, and Karen Blixen was never one to fight shy of a challenge.

Juma bin Mohamed, one of the unforgettable characters in Karen Blixen's portrait gallery of natives. Here he is with two kitchen *totos*, his own son "Tumbo" in the center.

96

What a small English boy of the upper class looked like in the nineties: Denys as a child.

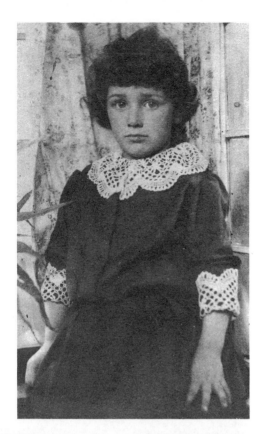

Opposite page: The record player that Denys Finch-Hatton gave Karen Blixen, and the album with Stravinsky's *Petroushka*, now at Rungstedlund. Beethoven's Piano Concerto No. 4 containing Kamante's favorite theme, the Andante, is there too.

Denys Finch-Hatton, the image of a young man with great reserves of body and mind to draw upon. This photograph was probably taken during his time at Oxford, where he had a reputation as a fine athlete. Among his books now at Rungstedlund is a dictionary of music which he received at Eton as a prize for singing. Both Denys and his friend Berkeley Cole considered singing a natural part of happy human relationships. The song "Where'er You Walk," to Händel's music, quoted by Karen Blixen in her *Bonfire Speech*, was one that Denys had sung to her.

Paintings by Karen Blixen, done in Africa in the twenties. Opposite page:
A toucan, a pitcher and an open book—Holberg's *History of Denmark*, which
she had brought with her to Africa. Above: A young Kikuyu *ndito* (virgin).
Page 102: Abdullahi Ahamed, a young cousin of Farah's, who was intelligent
and eager to be educated. In spite of hard times Karen Blixen and Farah managed, between them, to scrape together the fees to send him to the Moham-
medan school he wanted to attend. Later she sent him a typewriter which
became a help in his career. When she last heard from him, he was a judge in
Hargeisa in Somaliland. After Karen Blixen's death he turned to Thomas
Dinesen asking him for help to find someone who could assist him with the
English text of a book he is preparing about the history of the Somalis. Page
103: Ereri, an old Kikuyu.

A strangely shaped cloud above the Ngong Hills.—The cloud formations are mentioned in the poem "Ex Africa," written in Denmark in 1915, of the land she was longing to get back to—"clouds trailing shadows over Bardamat."

Opposite page: Karen Blixen on safari.—It is in pictures from this same safari that Karen and Bror's Swedish friend Baron Eric von Otter appears, the man who was called "Resase Modja" ("One Cartridge") because he never needed more for each head of game he aimed at.

Karen Blixen also undertook a safari alone with Africans, when her husband had volunteered at the outbreak of the war. It was not a pleasure expedition but transport for the government, and this particular safari held a special place in the memory of the people on the farm. It was on this occasion that a lion attacked an ox, and no rifle being at hand, Karen Blixen chased the lion away with a whip. It also happened during this single-handed enterprise that her camp was one day sighted by her husband's outfit and an eagle-eyed African reported to him that there was "a small bwana with white stones in his ears" outside the tent. It was, however, Tanne with the pearls she loved to wear at all times because they had been given to her by Daisy, her best friend.

Young Kikuyus dressed for a celebration.—The Africans' festive occasions played a great part in the life of the farm. Karen Blixen admired the way in which the dark people themselves, their dress and ornaments, and the whole African landscape formed a vast organic whole. She disapproved of the missionaries' endeavors to make the natives dress in European clothes. It seemed to her quite out of style, "like a harness on a lion or a giraffe."

One of the big dance festivals, a *ngoma*. As many as fifteen hundred guests sometimes came to the farm for these occasions. Invitations to such "balls" were very popular in the surrounding country. But only the day-time *ngomas* were purely social events. The night *ngomas* were "in earnest," writes Karen Blixen. They were held only after the corn harvest, and at full moon, and were an ancient ritual.

Gustav Lous Mohr (center) and Thomas Dinesen (right) with a third safari companion. About 1925.—Gustav Mohr was one of Karen Blixen's best friends in Africa, "a rousing farmer," who helped her, in word and deed, more than anyone else. He would often drop in and discuss politics, social problems and literature for many hours. He read nothing but contemporary literature. The new authors had read the old ones, he reasoned, therefore he could limit himself to the new books. Once when he was ill for a few days and laid up in Karen Blixen's house, she showed him D. H. Lawrence's latest novel but told him he could not have it until he had read the hundred-year-old Danish poem, by Oehlenschläger, of the god Thor angling for the Midgård serpent. He did, and admitted it was magnificent. Gustav Mohr was killed on December 27, 1936, while crossing a river in Tanganyika.

Karen Blixen, in 1923, with a tame owl she had for a while, and which liked to sit on her shoulder. The bird came to a sad end. It used to swallow bits of thread, as a substitute for what owls will swallow in their natural habitat, but one day it started on the cord of a window blind, from which it was discovered hanging dead. But the owl lives on in a small painting by Karen Blixen, owned by a relative.

Karen Blixen at the factory (below), where the coffee was processed. In this photograph, from the twenties, the factory is probably being rebuilt after a fire. There was a huge coffee drier, and the picturesque setting when the machine had to be emptied in the middle of the night is described in the book about the farm. A shipment on its way to the coffee auction in London represented a great deal of labor by the people on the farm, down to the little boys leading the oxen, sixteen to each wagon, into Nairobi and back. Left: Karen Blixen in her regular working clothes.

Berkeley Cole (1882–1925).—"Berkeley, if he had had his small head enriched with a wig of long silky curls, could have walked in and out of the Court of King Charles II," Karen Blixen writes of him. The inner man corresponded well to the outward. But in the chapter "Visitors to the Farm," she also says that where the jest was carried far, sometimes it became pathetic. Berkeley Cole and Denys Finch-Hatton, her two best English friends, thought of themselves as deserters from the modern world, but were more like exiles who bore their exile with a good grace. They would have cut a figure in any age and did cut a figure in their own time, but somehow did not belong to their century, Karen Blixen wrote of them.—Berkeley Cole, a couple of years older than Karen Blixen, was one of the very early settlers and was on especially friendly terms with the Masai. When he was staying at the farm, they came to see him. His jokes made them laugh, and "it was as if a hard stone had laughed." "When Berkeley died, the country changed"—"standards were lowered when he went."

Karen Blixen on horseback in front of the house, about 1922.—She
mentioned once that one of the dogs would not follow her when she
rode, only when she walked; in order to teach him, she was going to
take him along on a long leash—and thoughtlessly held the cord around
her hand while mounting. The dog threaded the cord around the horse's
legs, it nearly cut through the rider's fingers and she somersaulted to
the ground. Some of the native children were delighted spectators and
asked her to do it again.

Opposite page: On the doorstep with a big bouquet of lilies, about
1922.—Both in Africa and later at Rungstedlund, Karen Blixen was a
dedicated grower of flowers for bouquets. Her arrangements were
works of art, often quite unorthodox in that she would combine garden
flowers and wild flowers with things from the vegetable garden like
red-cabbage leaves and leek flowers. Often much work had gone into
the making, but she was not sorry to see them wilt after a few days;
on the contrary, she looked forward to making new ones.

Opposite page: Children of the farm playing with one of the big dogs. —Karen Blixen sometimes said that children are so awful that one can only put up with them because they are so small. But in practice, she simply could never resist playing with any children who were, at the moment or for a longer period, part of her surroundings. No doubt the little boy in the picture was encouraged to mount and sit like a fine horseman on Dusk, Pania or Askari. It must have been an everyday scene. Inevitably, the chapter called "Kitosch's Story" comes to mind, for comparison. A young African was flogged to death by his white employer for having mounted the owner's horse. When she included that incident in her book about Africa, Karen Blixen wanted to be on absolutely safe ground, so she arranged to have copied and sent to her from Kenya all the newspaper accounts of the court proceedings. The document still exists, many handwritten pages, possibly ordered from one of the professional letter writers whose services were available to those who had not learned to write.—It was to one of those letter writers that Kamante dictated: "Then your old farm it was good place for cow small calf black people." That letter, too, still exists.

Workers on the farm, photographed by Thomas Dinesen.

"A Biblical figure" it has been said of "Emmanuelson," the lonely traveler who came to the farm and left the next day, never to return. The chapter "A Fugitive Rests on the Farm" gives a fine and striking portrait of him. But later when Karen Blixen visited Stockholm, "Emmanuelson" telephoned her and was angry. His aunts, respectable ladies in a Swedish provincial town, had taken a dim view of her description of him. Karen Blixen then invited Casparson—that was his real name— to have dinner with her again, this time at Grand Hotel, and they had the same wine they had had for dinner on the farm, and were reconciled.—Casparson had seen much of the world since they last met; among other things, he had lived on a roof terrace in Cairo with a Sioux Indian girl. "How did she ever get to Cairo?" "On a bicycle," replied Casparson with the same ingenuousness as when, in the conversation on the farm, he had said, "Perhaps you will think me a terrible skeptic if I now say what I am going to say. But with the exception of God, I believe in absolutely nothing whatever."—Opposite page: A self-portrait found among Karen Blixen's papers at Rungstedlund. Below: Casparson's dedication.

Till Baronesse Blixen från Emanuelson

Opposite page: Twice during the twenties Ingeborg Dinesen undertook the long, uncomfortable journey to Africa to visit her daughter.
Denys Finch-Hatton admired her good English—a rarity among Danes
of that generation, but acquired thanks to her being partly of English
descent—and the native children were speechless at the sight of her
hair, which was so long that she could sit on it. During the Abyssinian
war the young African who had been Mrs. Dinesen's personal servant
during her stay wrote to Karen Blixen that if Old Memsahib had been
out there, people would not have permitted themselves such behavior.

Below: In 1925 Thomas Dinesen became engaged to Jonna Lindhardt,
daughter of Very Reverend Vincentz Lindhardt of Aarhus, and they
were married in April 1926. Here in the Morris on their first visit to
Mrs. Ingeborg Dinesen at Rungstedlund, August 13, 1925.

Karen Blixen at her desk, from which during all the years in Africa letters to her closest relatives, with interesting reports of daily life, made the long journey by ship and train to Denmark. Members of her family still treasure the many letters.

The warlike Masai, living next to the farm, caught Karen Blixen's interest from the first. Among the papers she left is a draft for an article about the Masai written in Africa.

A letter from Karen Blixen to Georg Brandes, dated Ngong, February 1926.—
As a young girl she had once sent him flowers. Mr. Brandes went to Rungstedlund to thank her in person, but was received by her mother only; Karen was
not permitted to meet him. In a letter from Africa to her Aunt Bess she blamed
her family for this incident, and said it had ruined her only chance at the time
for true intellectual development.—She had brought her early manuscripts
with her to Africa and continued writing. In the mid-twenties she attempted
a comeback in the Danish literary magazines. But fifteen years is a long time;
"Osceola" was forgotten. One isolated appearance of the name in connection
with the poem "Ex Africa" (*Tilskueren* magazine, 1925) had not been enough
to re-establish it. As a last resort Karen Blixen sent *The Revenge of Truth: A
Marionette Comedy*, to Georg Brandes, after she had arranged to meet and
speak with him during a visit to Denmark in 1925. "It is impossible for me
to get anything read and published by others without sending it to you," she
wrote (above). The play then appeared in *Tilskueren* in 1926, under the name
of Karen Blixen-Finecke (opposite page). Osceola was no more, Karen Blixen-
Finecke had made her first appearance. The name became even more short-
lived than Osceola; a second marionette comedy mentioned in correspondence
was never published.

SANDHEDENS HÆVN

En Marionetkomedie.

Af Karen Blixen-Finecke

———

Personerne:

Abraham, en bedragersk Krovært.

Sabine, hans Datter.

Jan Bravida, en ung Landsknægt og Journalist, Gæst i Kroen.

Mopsus, Kældersvend.

Fortunio, Piccolo.

Amiane, en omvandrende Kone, som egentlig er en Slags Fe eller Hex.

Handlingen foregaar i Abrahams Kro.

1ste Scene.

Abraham. Kære Mopsus, slaa Jan Bravida ihjel for mig inat. Nu er det længe siden, at jeg har bedt Dig om at slaa nogen ihjel, min kære Mopsus, nu kan Du ikke sige, at det er for meget forlangt. Det bliver da mærkværdigt at tænke paa, Mopsus, at iaften er han levende og imorgen er han død. Iaften er Døden ikke i hans Hoved, imorgen er det fuldt af den og intet andet. O, i Sandhed jeg elsker Døden. Den er det eneste, vi har tilbage af de gamle Dages Storhed, og uden den kunde intet Menneske holde Livets Kedsommelighed ud. Hvilken Demokrat er Du ikke, Død, min Kammerat, som praktiserer den sande Lighed, o, lad alle Demokrater gaa hen og lægge sig, naar Døden kommer. „Hvad," siger Døden, „beklager I jer over, at Kong Ramses og Henry Ford har været rigere end I i 50 Aar, naar jeg skal gøre eders Indtægter lige store i de næste 5 Millioner Aar?" Han siger: „Taler I om Fremtidsstater, Børn? Skændes ikke, skændes ikke herom. Min Fremtidsstat er eders alles Fremtid, og jeg skal bære eder dertil." „Jeg skal lære eder Broderskab Brødre," siger Døden, „den ene skal ikke have Hovedet højere end den anden, og der skal ikke være et ondt Ord imellem jer. Saa bliver da," siger Døden, „Frihed, Lighed og Broderskab, disse tre, men størst iblandt disse er Broderskab" og endnu en Gave har Demokraternes Forbillede, Døden, det er Stilhed. Hvilken Lettelse bliver det ikke, naar vi engang alle tier stille. Vent til han sover, Mopsus, vent til han sover. Ja, bær Dig nu forstandig ad. Jeg selv har ogsaa en Forretning at gøre med Meindert Hobtoma, en god Forretning. Ak, var Du kun lidt forstandigere.

Mopsus. Jeg beklager mig ikke, Herre, over min Forstand, men jeg er ked af, at jeg ikke er mere dristig, jeg er desværre saa nervøs, Herre, bare ved det, I nu har sagt, er jeg helt ude af Ligevægt. For et saadant Menneske er det i Grunden ogsaa et Fejlgreb at blive Tyv og Morder, hvad der skal foregaa i Mørke,

While in Africa, Karen Blixen had an audience and a contact with intellectual life, mainly in the person of Denys Finch-Hatton. In one of the first chapters of *Out of Africa* she relates: "I began in the evenings to write stories, fairy tales and romances, that would take my mind a long way off, to other countries and times. I had been telling some of the stories to a friend when he came to stay on the farm." He would sit on the floor with all the cushions spread around him, and listen attentively to a long tale from beginning to end. He taught her Latin, and to read the Bible and the Greek poets. His Bible, which accompanied him on all his journeys, is now at Rungstedlund, where it was photographed next to the old typewriter Karen Blixen used in Africa and for another thirty years after her return to Denmark, up to the last weeks before her death. She could never get used to any other.

Karen Blixen and her favorite dog, Pania, photographed on the terrace in the late twenties.

The road tow Pisa.

Herman von Spiegelhausen, a
young poet of ... Herr, was
travelling in Italy in the spring
of 1822. He was in ... today
driving from place to place
in search of peace of mind as
happiness, which he was so
...

One fine may cross he stopped
at a little inn on the road to
Pisa. — The air was clear as
clear as filled with sheet ...
and ... ... deeper light,
a lot of swallows were ...
about in it. While they made
his supper was Herman
walked down the road, along which
a big row of big poplars grew,

A first draft, in English, of the opening lines of "The Roads Round Pisa."—No purpose would be served by belaboring these summary captions with scholarly notes, but it is worth noting that important light is thrown on this particular manuscript by the Danish literary critic Aage Kabell in his book *Karen Blixen debuterer* (Karen Blixen Makes Her Debut), 1968. With gently wry sympathy he gives an account of Karen Blixen's vain attempt at a comeback in Danish literature. Among the unpublished manuscripts there is a notebook of English make, evidently bought in Nairobi, different from the early Danish notebooks that she had with her in Africa, and in it is the beginning of a marionette comedy *in English*. A little later she decided to work out the theme as a story instead. It exists in its full length, is called *Carnival*, and was originally intended for inclusion in a volume of nine tales, but it was eventually left out, as was, temporarily, "The Caryatids."—In Denmark there were no open doors, no one was interested—and so it came about that in the fullness of time, when life had brought Karen Blixen to the point where she devoted herself seriously to writing, it was in English and with encouragement and advice from Denys Finch-Hatton that she set to work.

A picture from 1930, the year before she left the farm. Farah stands on the left, the smallest boy is his son Saufe.—When the girls school now housed in Karen Blixen's old home was inaugurated in 1963, the radio broadcast included an interview with the grown-up Saufe, who was heard to say, "I was the first African child carried by a white." On the right are Juma, who was half Masai, and Juma's son who used to be called "Tumbo."

Somali women on the farm.—When Farah married and brought his young bride, Fathima, from Somaliland, her mother, her younger sister and a young cousin came with her, and Karen Blixen had a house built for them. The older woman taught the young ones etiquette and exquisite manners. The aim was to fetch the highest possible price in the marriage market. Karen Blixen spent much time in the company of the graceful, risible young ladies, and discussed everything with them, from theology to clothes. The young cousin was married on the farm; the wedding lasted for seven days. The small boy on the left is Farah's son Saufe, born toward the end of Karen Blixen's time on the farm. When he was a tiny infant "swaddled like an acorn," she borrowed him to take to bed like a doll, to allay her anguish and grief over the tragedy which was inexorably drawing near: that she must lose the farm.

Fishing in a river, in the late twenties.

Opposite page: Karen Blixen and two Africans plodding through a forest, in 1929. While the early pictures show a well-fed European, compared to the lean Africans, at this stage illness and worry had brought about a noticeable assimilation.

Africans crowding around Denys Finch-Hatton's small Gypsy-Moth airplane, which he used as a means for planning his safaris. He was a perfectionist when it came to using the best possible equipment for whatever he was doing. Airplanes were still comparatively rare in Africa in the twenties, and the small aircraft took on great importance for the people of the farm, who seemed to feel it belonged to all of them. In one of the drawings made by children on the farm, evidently with materials given to them by Karen Blixen, the plane is seen in the air above the house. The aerial photos of the farm on pages 132 and 137 were taken by Denys Finch-Hatton.—Flying over the African highlands must have influenced Karen Blixen's intellectual and spiritual development to a degree that can hardly be exaggerated.

On Friday, May 8, 1931, Denys Finch-Hatton flew from the farm for
the last time. He said he would be back the following Thursday. Just
before his departure he had had one of those spells of absent-minded-
ness which usually meant some kind of foreboding. The African whom
he asked to accompany him from Mombasa to Voi refused, and later
said, "Not for a hundred rupees would I, then, have gone up with
Bwana Bedâr." Karen Blixen was waiting for him on Thursday, the
fourteenth, but he did not come. His plane had crashed and he was
killed. — The picture of him at Voi (opposite page, bottom) is probably
the last one taken of him, and was sent to Karen Blixen after his death.

To the Baroness of
Blixen — in
remembrance of
Days —
Voi: 1931.   Longford:

Obituary from *The Times* (of London), 1931.

CAPTAIN FINCH-HATTON

AN APPRECIATION

A correspondent writes:–

To many of every type and station in life in many parts of the world the death of Denys Finch-Hatton means the loss of something that can never be replaced. All through his life he had an amazingly attractive personality: no one who ever met him, whether man or woman, old or young, white or black, failed to come under his spell, and one and all were proud to know him.

He was different from every one else. Always and everywhere absolutely himself, he was neither selfish nor self-centred, yet he seemed always to do everything that he wanted to do and never to do anything that he did not want. Anyone else, leading such a life, would have deteriorated; he remained considerate, sympathetic, humorous, cultured, and always had time somehow to spend in small acts of kindness for most unlikely people of any age or type. He was an ideal companion at the Russian Ballet or at a game of chess, while, of course, in times of difficulty or danger in the open air he was obviously supreme, the direct, ready master of the situation.

What in others might seem odd, even swagger, in him was absolutely natural, simple, and genuine. From some unpronounceable and possibly illegible address in the wilds of Africa he wrote long letters, chiefly about the books he was reading. He was a skilful mechanic and a lover of poetry and music; he had a wide and first-hand knowledge of birds and animals, and he was a shrewd observer of his fellow men and women. He could talk for hours of native life and customs, in which he was deeply interested, and hes knowledge and experience of the people and country and his intensely practical schemes have already been of great service to the Government.

He always left an impression of greatness – there is no other word – and aroused interest as no one else could. It was not only his magnificent physique and striking features; there was the ready intuition and sympathy with every type of character, a wonderful sense of humour, a complete lack of all sham or conventionality, a sense of power and determination; and yet behind it all, indefinite but ever present, a feeling of waste. Something more must come from one so strong and gifted; and in a way it did, for no one inspired more love and admiration, truer or deeper confidence or friendship.

He died, as he would have chosen, in the open air, amid the wide spaces that he loved, fearless and free to the end; and the charm of his wonderful personality and companionship is something which those who knew him will treasure throughout their lives.

The obelisk on the grave in the Ngong Hills.—Denys Finch-Hatton's brother, the Earl of Winchilsea, who had always admired his gifted younger brother, had it set up and chose the inscription. After Karen Blixen left Africa, Gustav Mohr wrote to her of a strange phenomenon at the grave: a lion and a lioness would come and stand or lie on the grave for a long time. Nothing could have been more fit and decorous, she thought, and there are many who will remember her added reflection, which ends the chapter "Farewell to the Farm": "Lord Nelson himself . . . in Trafalgar Square, has his lions made only out of stone."

The bronze plaque on the obelisk, with name and dates and the lines out of Coleridge's "The Ancient Mariner," one of Denys' favorite poems.

DENYS GEORGE FINCH HATTON

1887~1931

"HE PRAYETH WELL WHO LOVETH WELL
BOTH MAN AND BIRD AND BEAST"

Even before Denys Finch-Hatton's death, Karen Blixen had been packing and getting everything ready for her departure. Some of the furniture ended up in the memorial library (above) which Lady Macmillan was building in remembrance of her deceased husband, Sir Northrup Macmillan. The most difficult part by far of the winding up was to find land elsewhere for the squatters so they could stay together. She carried on endless negotiations with the authorities over this question. And it was not forgotten; when Jomo Kenyatta was a student in London, he remembered it and mentioned it to his Danish friend Peter P. Rohde, sending her at the same time an inscribed copy of his article about the religion of the Kikuyu people. The shareholders, relatives who had invested in the Karén Coffee Company, lost much money on this African venture and in the end had to call a halt. The consortium which bought the farm and broke it up into building lots undoubtedly made a good profit. But to partake in that stage would have been impossible for Karen Blixen, because it would have meant driving her African people away from the land they regarded as their own while she herself exploited it. She had always been loyal to them, and when she gave them corn out of her own provisions in the bad years, she did not insist on being paid back in better times, a policy the other farmers characterized as unrealistic. —Farah, who had met her in Aden and accompanied her to Mombasa in 1914, now escorted her from the farm down to Mombasa, and from the ship she watched his figure on the quay grow smaller and smaller and at last disappear.

Dear Friend,

I send you many greetings. Whatever you do, remember the country you love and the natives in the country.

Writer
Jomo Kenyatta

Kwa Rafiki ....
Nakutumia Salamu Nyingi,
yote ufanyayo Kumbuka nchi
Unayoipenda na wenyeji Wakoimo.

Mwandishi
Jomo Kenyatta
3rd. August 1937.

Thomas Dinesen went down to meet his sister in Marseilles, where the S/S *Mantola* arrived on August 19, 1931. All was lost. There was one little incident from their reunion which she never forgot. To her annoyance her stockings were sagging—in the graphic Danish phrase she used, they were "hanging in eels"—and Thomas simply suggested that they go to a shop and buy a new pair of garters, which they did. The fact that this depressing little nuisance could easily be remedied gave her a first glimpse of hope.—Being bankrupt and forced to find a way to make a living, she chose to continue working on the stories she had begun writing in English. She had to ask Thomas to support her for two years, moved into her mother's home at Rungstedlund, with two rooms at her personal disposal—her father's study, and the paneled room in the attic, which Thomas had used as a young man—and worked for two years on the book, but without any contact, let alone contract, with a publisher.

One of her mother's friends sent a jubilant note, quoting a popular poem about the prodigal daughter who was at last safely back, and one of her girlhood friends had stood in the window when the van with the boxes from Africa swung into the yard. They were stowed away in the attic, and not until thirteen years later was she in a mood for unpacking. Only the books and manuscripts which she needed were brought out. The old French wooden

138

screen (page 140) with painted figures of Chinamen, sultans, and Negroes with dogs on leashes, used to stand by the fire, and in the evening the fire had made the pictures stand out and serve as illustrations to the tales she told Denys. She had looked at the screen for a long time before packing it, and probably it was one of the few objects that emerged from the boxes before she set to work at her father's old desk.

"First things first" was ever a maxim of Karen Blixen's, and during the two years when it was a matter of life and death for her to get her book written, it became a problem to restrict her participation in the family life across the hall, where a grandmother's heart was gladdened by the visits of grandchildren, and other relatives came and went. But there was no mistaking the warm welcome given to the prodigal daughter, and much was sacrificed to enable her to concentrate on her task.

Mrs. Ingeborg Dinesen with her first grandchild, Ea Neergaard's daughter Karen, and Jonna Lindhardt, Thomas Dinesen's fiancée, on the steps at Rungstedlund, August 1925.

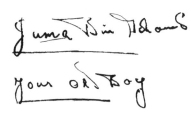

Juma bin Mohamed. — When Karen Blixen went back to live in Denmark again, she considered calling herself "Mrs. Dinesen." This, however, would have been unpractical, for various reasons. "My African people would not have known me or been able to find me under that name," she said. So she remained "the Baroness," to the irritation of some. Her contact with the people of the farm continued except for the interruption during the Second World War. — This picture was sent to her by Juma, who wrote on the back: "Juma bin Mohamed your old boy."

Malla Jørgensen, who had come to Rungstedlund about 1894 as nanny to Thomas and Anders Dinesen. Here about 1930, toward the end of her life, with Thomas Dinesen's two daughters, Anne and Ingeborg. — When Karen Blixen was invited to write an article about "the most unforgettable character I ever met," she proposed Farah or Malla, but neither suggestion was accepted. (She wrote of Farah elsewhere, but never about Malla.)

Opposite page: A passport photograph, the first that Karen Blixen had taken after her return to Denmark. At the outbreak of the Abyssinian war in 1936 she was hoping her success as a writer would get her a job as a war correspondent which would take her back to Africa. She was hired by a London newspaper, but the assignment was canceled lest there be too much trouble if a woman correspondent came to grief in the perilous undertaking. Shortly thereafter she found an opportunity to observe negotiations at the League of Nations in Geneva.

Karen Blixen kept her word and *Seven Gothic Tales* was ready in two years, by the middle of 1933. But a bitter disappointment awaited her: the publisher to whom she got herself introduced in London did not even want to look at the manuscript. She returned home without having accomplished anything. In the desperate situation, after several refusals, Thomas Dinesen stepped in again, finding an expert who was willing to read the manuscript: the author Dorothy Canfield, whom he had met at Kastrup Airport and driven to Folehave to visit Mary Bess Westenholz. She fell "under its spell," and advised her friend Robert K. Haas to publish it. He said: "This won't sell but it is too good not to publish." The book was received with enthusiasm and was the Book-of-the-Month Club selection for February 1934.

Hard-earned and well-earned success, it would seem. But rightly or wrongly, Karen Blixen got the impression that within the family it had to be played down in order not to hurt the feelings of her sister Ellen Dahl, whose books had not enjoyed a similar success. Nevertheless, it was the publishing firm of Reitzel, owned by Ellen Dahl's husband, Knud Dahl, which brought out the Danish edition a year later, after Karen Blixen herself had translated the book into Danish (above, right).

144   Opposite page: Kehlet's photograph of Karen Blixen in 1934, which became widely known, as it was published in America after the identity behind the pseudonym of Isak Dinesen had been revealed.

In connection with the publication of the Danish version of *Seven Gothic Tales* in 1935, a celebration was held in Copenhagen in honor of Karen Blixen, or rather Isak Dinesen. She is seen here sitting between her mother and the author Otto Rung.—Mrs. Ingeborg Dinesen too had earned the right to celebrate; it had not been easy for her to keep things quiet enough at Rungstedlund to allow Tanne to work in peace during those many months—then she had been "Tanne" again. No one in Denmark knew "Tania," as she had been known to her English friends, and at the time there was as yet no "Isak Dinesen" or "Karen Blixen."

Karen Blixen had prepared a big surprise for her mother's eightieth birthday on May 5, 1936. She had bought a used car but a very fine one, and it was parked in front of the house with a sign reading "Chauffeur Isak at your service for one hour daily," and at the wheel she had placed a dummy dressed in the splendid coat which in the old days had been worn by Alfred Pedersen, the coachman.

Brøndum's Hotel in Skagen. When Karen Blixen was working on her next book, *Out of Africa*, her mother had a period of illness which caused a serious delay in her schedule. In order to meet the publisher's deadline, she loaded her small car with manuscript and typewriter as soon as she possibly could and fled to the farthest end of the country to find a place where she would be able to concentrate on her writing. First she stayed at Brøndum's Hotel and later, when the hard winter of 1936–37 set in, she moved to the smaller Skagen's Hotel, run by Mrs. Østergaard. The cold was excruciating but the work was going well, and she even found time to make new friends and feel at home in the town. At one point, however, she was completely at a loss: she agonized over whether the section entitled "From an Immigrant's Notebook" was any good and whether it should be included in the book, so she persuaded Thomas Dinesen to come to Skagen and help her. In his opinion it was good and should be included. The American literary critic Robert Langbaum, who has published a major study of her work, agrees with Thomas Dinesen and demonstrates in his book how appropriate it is that this part is placed between "Visitors to the Farm" and the last act of the tragedy.

The drawing for the cover of *Out of Africa,* used both in England by Putnam and in the United States by Random House. After the original which is now at Rungstedlund.—Karen Blixen herself preferred the cover of the first Danish edition, after an African drawing which had been given to her as a present by Esa, her cook, and which is mentioned in the book.

149

Professor Hartvig Frisch (1893–1950).—Rungsted, as it had developed during the years Karen Blixen lived in Africa, seemed to her to have become a tedious place to live. In her early youth when there were fewer people in the neighborhood, they knew each other better. But she did find a small number of new friends in Rungsted and Hørsholm after her return, and one of the best was Hartvig Frisch, classical scholar and a leading figure in the Social-Democratic party, for some years Minister of Education. The conversations she had with him were of great importance to her, and one of them led directly to her writing "Sorrow-acre." Hartvig Frisch was also one of the friends she invited to meet her relative by marriage, Count Erich Bernstorff-Gyldensteen, who spent some time each winter at a nearby health resort; she enjoyed bringing together, in her home, people of widely different views and backgrounds.

Johannes V. Jensen (1873–1950), awarded the Nobel Prize for Literature in 1944. — A quotation from one of his poems was used by Karen Blixen in *Out of Africa* to express a central idea: "Noble found I/ever the Native,/and insipid the Immigrant." She admired his writing, and they met sometimes in the homes of mutual friends, one of whom was Hart-vig Frisch. — In a letter to Karen Blixen dated November 16, 1942, Johannes V. Jensen said that her work gave him a sense of liberation and re-creation, that it is characterized by a soaring imagination and artistic composition, and that she qualifies to be called a poet.

WILHELM DINESEN
19 DECEMBER 1845
28 MARTS 1895
INGEBORG DINESEN
WESTENHOLZ
DIN MISKUNDHED GUD
TROFASTHED
DINE

Karen Blixen in the drawing room at Rungstedlund (above). The photograph was probably taken during the period between the publication of *Out of Africa* in 1937 and the death of her mother in January 1939.

Opposite page: The grave of her parents in the Hørsholm Cemetery.

Karen Blixen during a conversation (right). Detail from a press photo, about 1940.—She once remarked, "One of the things in my life I have been unhappy about is that I was not better-looking than I actually was. On the other hand, one of the things I have been pleased about is that at least I was as good-looking as I actually was." On another occasion, when complimented on her looks by an acquaintance, she replied, "Well, I did attend art school in Paris, you know."

153

In 1939, Karen Blixen had planned to go on a pilgrimage to Mekka together with Farah Aden and his mother, but the outbreak of the war prevented the realization of this journey. To avoid being confined to Denmark she arranged with *Politiken* (a leading Danish daily) to write articles from London, Paris and Berlin. She was in Berlin from March 1 to April 2, 1940—choosing to get the most precarious part over with first—and the German occupation of Denmark put a stop to the rest. She is photographed here in the company of confirmed Nazis who are trying to convert her. She was to have an audience with Hitler, but when given to understand that she ought to send him in advance an inscribed copy of one of her books, she caught a cold and had to cancel the appointment.

Opposite page: One of the finest examples of contemporary Danish graphic art is *Rungstedlund—A Garden*, by Erik Clemmesen, published in 1941 in twenty-five copies. It was thanks to a personal friendship that this book was produced: at the beginning of the century there existed a warm friendship between the family of Rungstedlund and the Ahlefeldt-Laurvig family of Flakvad, about half a mile farther south. The marriage of Count Ahlefeldt's younger daughter, Christine, to Erik Clemmesen became the link which connected the artist with Rungstedlund, and it was during his stay at Rungstedlund in the summer of 1940 that he completed the collection of etchings of the park.

RUNGSTEDLUND

EN HAVE

Indholdsfortegnelse

FREMSTILLET I 25 EXEMPLARER, HVORAF DETTE ER Nº
Pligtexemplar. uden Nº
KJØBENHAVN

Opposite page: At Rungstedlund.—Karen Blixen was very hospitable, and since she did not want her guests to have to stand by the door and wait for the bell to be answered, she looked for them through the window and was thus ready to receive them when they arrived.

During the hard winters of the war, Karen Blixen wrote *Winter's Tales*. After the tour de force of *Seven Gothic Tales*, and after *Out of Africa*, to which she had given her life's blood, she now turned to the moods and the themes of her youth for material. In spite of the ice-bound Sound, the blackout and the occupation troops outside, and frozen water pipes and an empty pantry inside (she flatly refused to do any hoarding), she went on writing. She did everything she could to have *Winter's Tales* published in England and the United States simultaneously with the publication of *Vinter-Eventyr* in Denmark, and she succeeded, although she did not know this until the war was over, when an American officer brought her a copy of the Armed Services edition, designed to fit into the pocket of a uniform. Through the Red Cross she received letters of thanks from readers on whom the book had made a deep impression. American soldiers, scattered all over the world, would receive "escape" literature from home, but in one of the letters to Karen Blixen the correspondent explained that to him her book, read in the Philippines, had been much more than that.

802

Winter's Tales

SHORT STORIES BY
ISAK DINESEN

Overseas edition for the Armed Forces. Distributed by the Special Services Division, A.S.F., for the Army, and by the Bureau of Naval Personnel for the Navy. U. S. Government property. *Not for sale.* Published by Editions for the Armed Services, Inc., a non-profit organization established by the Council on Books in Wartime.

ARMED
SERVICES
EDITION

THIS IS THE COMPLETE BOOK—NOT A DIGEST

The Ewald commemoration at Rungstedlund, June 11, 1943. — The great lyrical poet Johannes Ewald lived at Rungsted Inn, the present-day Rungstedlund, from 1773 to 1776, and his name is forever linked with the place. In the summer of 1943, two hundred years after Ewald's birth, several people at Rungstedlund decided to arrange an open-air festival in the park. Karen Blixen sanctioned the idea, became active in the preparations, and spoke in a moving way of the great poet and his connection with Rungsted (opposite page). — Born and bred in the same house, it was only natural that Karen Blixen should give him a place in her stories. He appears in "The Supper at Elsinore" and is one of the two main characters in "Converse at Night in Copenhagen." — The old etching of Ewald's Hill used to have its place in "Ewald's Room," Karen Blixen's study at Rungstedlund, supposed to have been occupied by Ewald while he was staying at the inn.

EWALDSHÖI

After her return to Denmark, Karen Blixen had resumed contact—to the extent that her work and health allowed it—with her girlhood friends, especially the two Frijs sisters who were living in Denmark: Inger and Sophie (married to Count Erich Bernstorff-Gyldensteen) and their families. Karen Blixen is seen here at Wedellsborg with Count Julius Wedell, his wife Inger and their son Tido.

The large hospitable homes of Wedellsborg and Gyldensteen provided Karen Blixen with opportunities not only of spending her holidays there but also of bringing along her work. She wrote parts of her books there. She loved the salt meadows of Gyldensteen and the approach to the inner court through the yard surrounded by beautiful old farm buildings, and at Wedellsborg (above) she especially enjoyed the feeling of spaciousness created by the huge forests and the long beach that belonged to the estate.

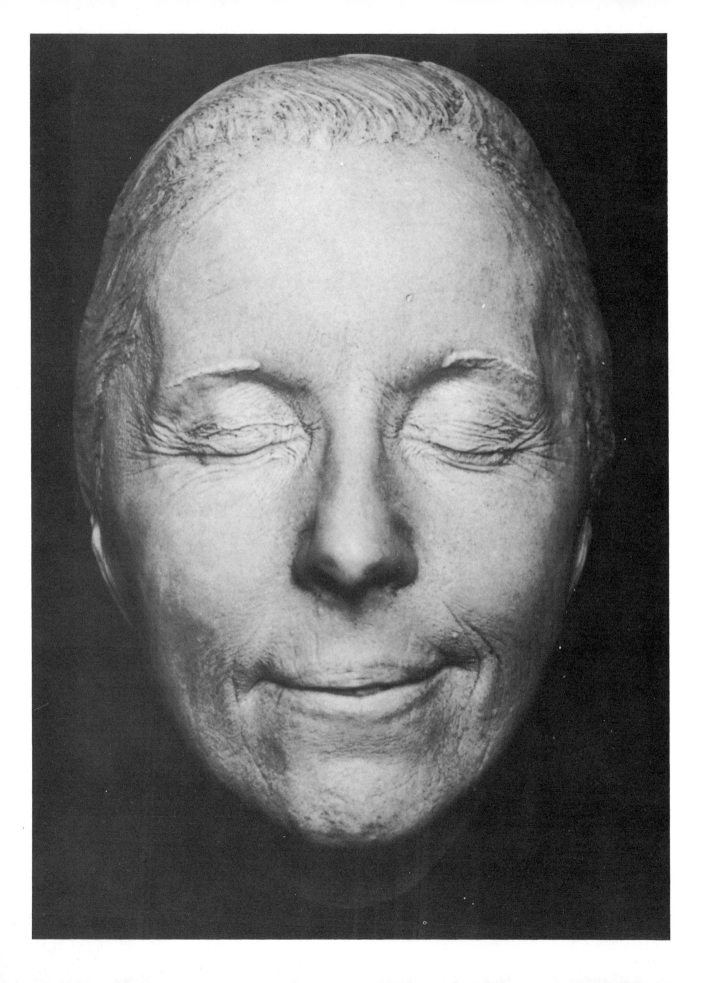

Opposite page: Life mask of Karen Blixen, made by the dentist Holger Winther, about 1940, and now in the Frederiksborg Museum. The photograph below was taken about the same time by the photographer Johannes Övereng in Hørsholm. Another photo by Övereng from this time was used on the identity card which was compulsory during the occupation, and which Karen Blixen compares, in *Shadows on the Grass*, to the detested *kipanda* which the European overlords forced on the Africans.

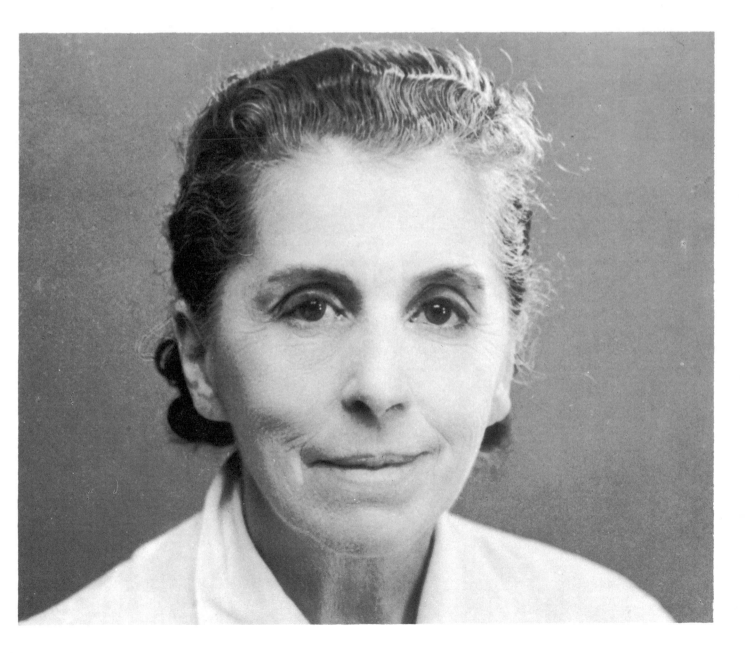

At the sundial, north of the house, Karen Blixen planted "eight-o'clock flowers" brought to her from northern Schleswig by her sister Ellen Dahl. The buds three inches long would burst around eight o'clock in the evening so rapidly that within a few minutes you could watch the whole process from tightly furled bud to full-blown flower. To Karen Blixen, more than half the pleasure of this rare phenomenon was to show it to her guests on a summer evening.

Karen Blixen on the footbridge over the pond, probably in 1943 because about that time she wore her hair tied with a bow at the back, which gave her a certain resemblance to her eighteenth-century predecessor at Rungstedlund, the poet Ewald. Another thing which helps date the picture is the curtains in the windows. Until her death in 1939 Mrs. Ingeborg Dinesen had her bedroom in the west wing. From 1944 it became the guest apartment, with a view of the lawns and the pond. It was the door here at the back of the house to which certain friends of Karen Blixen's in the resistance movement had keys during the war, and it became routine to remove the inner key from the lock at night.

Visiting Otto Rung at his summer place in northern Zealand. From left to right, top row: Professor Niels Bohr, the nuclear physicist; authors Christian Rimestad, Otto Rung and Aage Dons; Niels Bohr's son Hans; and Christian Rimestad's daughter Gerda (wearing her undergraduate cap). Front row: Mrs. Eva Rimestad; a relative of Otto Rung's; and Niels Bohr's wife, Margrethe. Center: Karen Blixen.—She loved to ride a bicycle, and until the last, irrevocable breakdown of her health at the age of seventy, would cover long distances. Wherever she went, youngsters would admire her magnificent, sporty-looking bicycle with a handlebar watch as its crowning glory.

Karen Blixen began to write a thriller during the German occupation. She did this for two reasons: first, as a reaction against the pressure and tensions of the times, and second, because no transfers could be made from America and England of her author's royalties, which constituted her principal income. She found herself in the same position as in Africa, and it almost came to the point of selling Rungstedlund (which she owned jointly with her brothers). She did, however, manage to hold out—for one thing thanks to the thriller, *The Angelic Avengers*, published in Denmark in 1944 (below)—until bank transfers from abroad were again possible. However, the amount she finally received had been reduced to one tenth of the original sum because she had to pay taxes, including a wartime surtax, both at home and abroad; she must have been the Danish author hardest hit by the double taxation (which was abolished shortly after the war). In spite of the book's success— it too was a Book-of-the-Month Club selection when it was finally brought out in America—Karen Blixen did not admit to being the author until many years later. She had used a new pseudonym, Pierre Andrézel.

HERETICA

TIDSSKRIFT REDIGERET
AF THORKILD BJØRNVIG
OG BJØRN POULSEN

76 SIDER
KR. 3.50

NR. 4
1. AARG.
1948

WIVEL

During the war Karen Blixen had become acquainted with the young
poet Ole Wivel (born 1921). He and his friend Knud W. Jensen would
look in now and then—once giving the old coachman, Alfred Pedersen,
an interesting day in dreary times by arriving on horseback. The mis-
tress of the house was of course equally interested in the two friends'
"stable" of promising young authors, whom they provided with a
publishing outlet for their work, first through Wivel's own publishing
house and later through Gyldendal, with which Wivel's Forlag merged
in 1954. She welcomed them in an open and friendly manner, and
among her guests were the first two editors of the new literary magazine
Heretica, Thorkild Bjørnvig and Bjørn Poulsen, as well as occasionally
the subsequent editors Tage Skou-Hansen and Frank Jæger, and more

often, later on, Jørgen Gustava Brandt, poet and essayist. The first and the last of the six volumes of *Heretica* had contributions by Karen Blixen: "Letters from a Country at War" and "Converse at Night in Copenhagen."

Below: The poet Thorkild Bjørnvig and Karen Blixen with Knud W. Jensen's dog Trofast (Faithful), about 1950.—Thorkild Bjørnvig had been awarded the Copenhagen University gold medal for a treatise on Rainer Maria Rilke and the German tradition, and for his master's degree in 1947 he had assiduously studied the great works of world literature, not only read about them; he was a perfect conversation partner for Karen Blixen, who was widely read herself and had an exceptional memory. Thus began a friendship which for a time meant much to both of them and was a mutual source of inspiration. Bjørnvig is one of the most important lyrical poets in postwar Denmark.

In "The Dreamers," one of the *Seven Gothic Tales*, it is said of Pellegrina Leoni that her fate was to put on, figuratively speaking, "her richest attire to meet the prince at a great ball, only to find that what she has been invited to is a homely gathering . . . at which everyday clothes are worn." But gala occasions did occur in the life of Pellegrina's creator. Here with fellow author Thit Jensen at the farewell party for Miss Ingeborg Andersen, president of Gyldendal, January 20, 1954.

Jørgen Claudi with the microphone at Rungstedlund, 1952.—Sometime in the late forties, Karen Blixen had been invited to speak at a meeting of the librarians' association in Copenhagen, and she told the story of Farah. Jørgen Claudi, a librarian who was at that time entering upon a career in Danish broadcasting, was also present at the meeting, and he persuaded Karen Blixen to repeat the story on the radio. Whereas her radio recital on the occasion of her father's centennial in 1945 had been an isolated occurrence, the informal talk on Farah became the first in a series which was very well received and brought her many gratifying reactions from the listeners. "Daguerreotypes" (in 1951) was pure entertainment; at other times she discussed subjects she felt strongly about: in 1954 about the ethical problems of using animals for experiments, and in 1958 about the future of Rungstedlund. It was also on the radio that some of her lighter stories which had been published in American magazines were first presented in Danish: "The Uncertain Heiress," read by Inge Hvid-Møller in 1951; "Babette's Feast," translated by Jørgen Claudi and read by Bodil Ipsen in 1950; "The Ghost Horses," read by Ingeborg Brams, also in 1950.—Below: Claudi; Nils Carlsen, the housekeeper's son, who six years later contributed to the broadcast on Rungstedlund and its bird sanctuary by playing an old song about the birds of the wood on his recorder; and Karen Blixen.

After the appearance of *The Angelic Avengers* in 1944, Karen Blixen encountered great obstacles in her path to the publication of her next book. The thirteen years until a volume of tales was ready in 1957 were interspersed with stays at the National Hospital, St. Lucas Hospital, the County Hospital at Hillerød, the Military Hospital, and the Municipal Hospital in Copenhagen; four operations and two treatments, which were, each in its own way, an ordeal; a fall, from sheer infirmity, down the whole length of the steep stairs in the hall at Rungstedlund; and attacks of pain and emesis which interrupted work, upset all plans and horrified her surroundings.

In spite of all this she persevered doggedly in her work, had to dictate more and more but in between did as much typing herself as possible, anywhere in the house, from the regular workroom to the bedroom, depending on where she would be most comfortable at the moment. In the winter she mostly used the two small guestrooms in the west wing (opposite page) because the larger rooms were often too cold to live in.

Now and then she was persuaded to let some smaller work be published, and in this way and through the radio broadcasts she kept in touch with her public. In 1952 a low-priced little book was published: *Babette's Feast* (see page 174), of which she also donated one royalty-free edition to be used as gifts for the subscribers to a new "popular library" of good entertainment which she approved of. The regular copies cost only one and a half krone and she opposed any price increase. In the same year an expensive and handsome publication also appeared: *The Cardinal's Third Tale*. When the booksellers' association announced that she would receive The Golden Laurels of the year, she took pleasure in the joke—as she saw it—and for the occasion put on a long white dress in Grecian style and a dark-green velvet cloak (see page 175); it was typical of her to choose an attire that matched the laurel wreath. (Later Mrs. Carlsen, her housekeeper, slipped into "Ewald's Room" one day and in an emergency picked a couple of leaves off it for cooking purposes.)

At long last everything looked more hopeful, a spell of fair wind, the interplay between author and public which was so important to her.

Then one day Eigil Christensen, the local bookseller, telephoned: Was it true that a new book of hers was about to be published, a novel written under another pseudonym? He had received advertising material to that effect. He let her have the material, and at the same time a well-prepared campaign of rumors and publicity was let loose in the press. The subject was a small novel, *An Evening in the Cholera Year*, of which she had never heard. The author was said to be Alexis Hareng. The advertising material sent out to booksellers included newspaper articles stating that "The Immortal Story," "also written by Karen Blixen," would be broadcast during November. Within a few days she was able to put two and two together. A fellow author, whom she had considered a friend and received as a guest in her house, was riding on the coattails of her publicity. It was later alleged that in writing the novel he had used a card index with characteristic words and stylis-

tic peculiarities copied from Karen Blixen's books, so that the result was a kind of synthetic Karen Blixen. Once in a radio interview he even borrowed an argument she had used in a discussion at a party in her home where he was one of the guests. On the farm the Africans had told her, "You don't get angry like other white people—you laugh!" and true to her own nature she set in motion a plan to end the incident which would have been a priceless joke. But a certain move from the other side made her afraid. She had a feeling that she was not in good

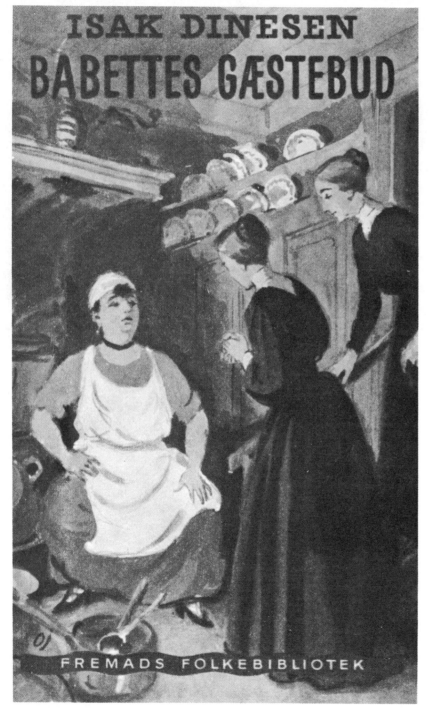

enough company to risk the joke, and that it would be interpreted
as a conspiracy between the two authors simply to create publicity
for each other. Depressed, and with her favorable working conditions
shattered for some time to come, she entered the next round: the County
Hospital, operation at the Military Hospital, the County Hospital again,
operation at the Municipal Hospital in Copenhagen.

Ingeborg Andersen, president of the Gyldendal publishing house (1887–1960). Publisher of Karen Blixen's works from and including *Out of Africa*. The inscription on the photograph reads: "To Karen with greetings from her three friends at Hannebjergvej: Binkie, Bonnie and Ingeborg, January 1954."—Ingeborg Andersen and the actor Erling Schroeder (the best Danish Hamlet) were the only two of her friends who called her by her given name. The qualities which Karen Blixen first and foremost valued in Ingeborg Andersen were her loyalty and her way of doing things in a big way.

Karen Blixen liked to show her stories while still in the manuscript stage to a select circle of relatives and trusted friends. The painter Erik Clemmesen belonged to that group. In 1952 one of the stories, *The Cardinal's Third Tale*, was published as a separate volume, with allusive drawings by Erik Clemmesen, who had done them during a sojourn in Rome for the purpose.

When Albert Schweitzer passed through Copenhagen in 1954 on his way to Oslo to receive the Nobel Peace Prize, it was a welcome opportunity for him and Karen Blixen to see each other again, although the stopover did not allow much time for their meeting. In London, in the thirties, Karen Blixen had sought his advice on hospital work in Africa; she had hoped that the income from her literary activities would enable her to establish and manage a children's hospital in the Masai Reserve.

Rungstedlund, in the mid-fifties.—By that time the hawthorn hedge screening off the house from the coast road had been replaced by a rose garden laid out by the landscape architect Georg Boye. The remaining part of the hedge was simply removed, to afford passers-by an unobstructed view of the lovely old lawns.

Opposite page: Many visitors to Rungstedlund remember as something special "the curtains sweeping the floor." The hanging of the summer curtains in the drawing room was the final touch to the big effort of spring-cleaning the sprawling old house. The tradition is still being kept up.

Opposite page: Karen Blixen posing in a Pierrot costume from her youth.

mc nissen-foto.

Karen Blixen and Alfred Pedersen.—He had come to Rungstedlund as a coachman when Tanne was ten, in 1895, and stayed there until his death sixty-five years later, when he was going on ninety. He was loyalty personified, primarily to Mrs. Ingeborg Dinesen, but he was also a big tease ("It's his Wendish blood," said Karen Blixen in jest— Alfred was from Lolland). He was middle-aged when he got his driver's license; if Karen Blixen was at the wheel with Alfred at her side, he would criticize her driving and give her instructions. He was also a great lover of animals, and a prominent member of the local rifle club. In his old age he sometimes felt lonely, and one of the things one remembers with gratitude is that shortly before his death Mrs. Carlsen, the housekeeper, declined an invitation to attend the performance at the Royal Theater celebrating the great actress Bodil Ipsen's fifty-year jubilee, because she wanted to keep her promise to Alfred Pedersen to accompany him to the jubilee of the rifle club. He died on January 13, 1960, just as the radical reconstruction of Rungstedlund was started.

Karen Blixen in Rome, May 1956.—Following the year 1955–56 when her health received the deathblow (a year which no one expected her to live through) Karen Blixen felt that a change of scenery would do her good and help her to restore contact with life, so arrangements were made for her to spend a week in Rome. A new friend was awaiting her there: the American writer Eugene Walter, who was an untiring and endlessly resourceful *maître de plaisir* for her in Rome in 1956, and again the following year.

When Karen Blixen made up a tentative table of contents for a new collection of stories called *Last Tales*, it saddened the hearts of the friends to whom she showed it—but it was not to be her last book. However, she had got used to the title and did not want to change it, even when it became apparent that it would be followed by other publications. She wanted this book to have a cover in colors of her own choosing and to incorporate the "golden section." She therefore consulted her friend and neighbor, Professor Steen Eiler Rasmussen, who designed the cover shown here.

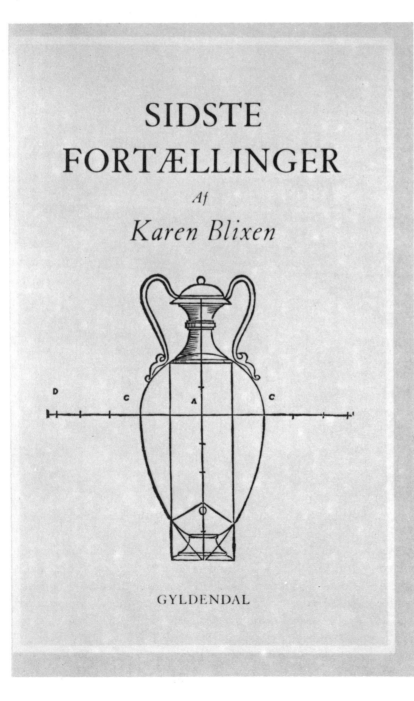

SIDSTE
FORTÆLLINGER
Af
Karen Blixen

GYLDENDAL

Ole Wivel and Karen Blixen at a reception held by Gyldendal on August 23, 1957, at the opening of the fall season during which *Last Tales* was published. In 1954 Ole Wivel had joined Gyldendal, together with Otto B. Lindhardt of the Wivel publishing house. He and Karen Blixen often differed in their views on a great many things, but their friendship of long standing was built upon a feeling of mutual confidence.

Opposite page: Karen Blixen signing her name in the visitors' book at the Caffè Greco in Rome, November 4, 1957. — Thirteen years had passed since *The Angelic Avengers*, and fifteen years since the last "real" book, *Winter's Tales*, but now at long last a new collection was ready, *Last Tales*, with enough stories left over to make up another volume the following year, *Anecdotes of Destiny*. This in itself was a great thing. Then, during 1957, strange things began to happen. A guest arrived from Stockholm, a well-known Swedish author who insisted that she grant him an interview, to be used later on; he was accompanied by a highly esteemed Danish photographer who took numerous pictures both inside and outside the house. The writer told Karen Blixen that he knew for a fact that the first voting of the Swedish Academy on the nominee for the Nobel Prize had resulted in a majority for her. Another interviewer telephoned from Oslo ("I know something of what is going on in Stockholm") and there was more of the same sort; rumors were rampant. Karen Blixen seemed to be quite unconcerned, but some trusting souls around her were naïve enough to be overjoyed at this unexpected thing happening just before her only book in many years was about to be published. Her publishers in other countries were delighted too, and some of them had already had posters printed. In the morning of October 17, it was impossible not to notice that Karen Blixen had about her some of that air of radiant expectancy which at times was apparent in her even until the very last days of her life; but the day before, she had said that there could be no substance to the rumors, since she had not been notified; a personal call from Stockholm had proved to be a trifling inquiry about a practical matter. In the evening of October 17, the radio news brought the official announcement that Albert Camus had been awarded the Nobel Prize.

In November, when *Last Tales* was published, Karen Blixen was in Rome. She had long before planned to be away at this time. A number of parties in her honor had been arranged on the initiative of Eugene Walter, and she was very happy in Rome, where in 1912 she had stayed with Daisy Frijs and her husband, Henrik Grevenkop-Castenskjold, the Danish ambassador. Perhaps her hosts were disappointed that it was not the Nobel Prize winner of the year they were entertaining, but fortunately, behind all these dazzling festivities, there was a genuine feeling of fondness and admiration for Karen Blixen, so it really did not matter. As far as the Americans among them were concerned, she was Isak Dinesen and to them would always remain Isak Dinesen.

The next stop after Rome was Paris, which Karen Blixen loved so well, and here too she felt happy. But it was Nancy Mitford's new book, and not *Last Tales*, that was on display in the bookshop windows. — The last week of the trip was spent in London, where Karen Blixen had old and loyal friends, above all Denys Finch-Hatton's two nieces Diana and Daphne. But when Karen Blixen saw her English publisher and was shown reviews, there were some that he left out, including one by Pamela Hansford Johnson, who took the opportunity to announce that in her opinion Karen Blixen was "the author who just missed it." In the United States, however, she was made an honorary member of the American Academy and the National Institute of Arts and Letters.

In the autumn of 1958, a man from the Swedish radio telephoned someone at the Danish radio who in turn called Rungstedlund and said that it was very important for his Swedish colleague to have some kind of recently taped statement by Karen Blixen in order to have everything ready, as there was a ninety-nine percent chance that she would get the Nobel Prize. The request was not passed on to Karen Blixen. In 1959, 1960 and 1961, brave voices could still be heard urging that it was high time. Karen Blixen's death in September 1962 spared her the embarrassment of once again being the rejected candidate. After her death the Belgian novelist Daniel Gillès wrote in an article about her: "Few epochs have been so radically mistaken as to their true literary values as ours."

Karen Blixen took a great interest in gardening, not only in the planning and supervision but also in the practical work. Here she is busy with the lopping shears removing suckers from the roses, which, out of consideration and generosity toward her fellow-men, she had substituted for the big hedge facing the Sound.

Each year when the hawthorn blossomed, Karen Blixen drove down to Dyrehaven, the large natural park near Klampenborg, to take a walk amid the largest concentration of hawthorn in the vicinity (opposite page). In the same way she just had to go to Fredensborg when the linden trees were in bloom. While Vilhelm Andersen, the great old man of Danish literary history, was still living she always paid him a visit on this occasion, and he used to say, "Now that the linden trees are in bloom, Karen Blixen will be here."

Karen Blixen getting ready for the day's work on a summer morning in "Ewald's Room" while Pasop is watching. She would start by re-reading and polishing off the work of the previous day. About 1956.

Opposite page: *Life* magazine had arranged with Karen Blixen to take pictures at Rungstedlund in November 1958. The result was a "close-up" covering two or three pages. It was still fresh in the minds of people she met during her visit to the United States in 1959, and was often the subject of conversation.

It was during these years that Karen Blixen rewrote her radio talk on Farah to form part of *Shadows on the Grass*, the small book of African memories published in 1960. Below is a draft of the final text.

og Verden, saa effektivt (formaalsbevidst) trængt
tilbage eller fortrængt af Tilværelsen, at den
hele Eksistensform tog sig ud, ikke alene som
enøjet, men som blind. Jeg følte de Befriede
ideer, g saa de uniformerede unge Mænd marchere
mod Fronten. For (oven) en Tramp er et Ralleskab, og
to Duellanter er en Enhed.
    Mit Møde med en anden Race, væsens-
forskellig fra min egen, blev i Afrika for mig
en mægtig og lykkelig Udvidelse af min Verden.
Lange skønne Klange tonede til alle Sider
om mig, min egen Stemme voksede, vgnste
g, og blev renere derved.—

As a token of gratitude after her radio appeal in 1958 (see next page) Karen Blixen planted the "Listeners' Oak," a sapling of an eight-hundred-year-old famous oak tree, on Ewald's birthday, November 18. She is being helped by the eminent forest botanist C. Syrach Larsen and P. Chr. Nielsen of the arboretum at Hørsholm.

The first meeting of the board of the Rungstedlund Foundation in the summer of 1958. Assembled in "Ewald's Room" are Karen Blixen (in the wing chair); Steen Eiler Rasmussen, professor of architecture; Knud W. Jensen, founder of the Louisiana Art Museum at Humlebæk; C. Syrach-Larsen, director of the arboretum at Hørsholm; Ingeborg Andersen, former president of Gyldendal; Karen Blixen's brother Anders Dinesen, one of the donators; Vagn Holstein, chairman of the Danish Ornithological Association; and Philip Ingerslev, attorney.

The foundation was built on two large gifts. Karen Blixen, her sister and younger brother donated the 40-acre estate of Rungstedlund, without receiving any compensation for the preservation of the park as a haven for the public in an otherwise highly developed area; and in addition, Karen Blixen donated the royalties and other income from her books in perpetuity. The reserve fund of 85,000 Danish kroner which originated from a much publicized radio appeal was, of course, a small gift in comparison, but it gave Karen Blixen particularly great pleasure. Some years later this special sum was rounded off to 100,000 through some American gifts, as a result of an article in *Vogue* magazine which Karen Blixen herself did not live to see published.

The object of the foundation is to preserve Rungstedlund as a private institution, to maintain a bird sanctuary on the property, and to make the main building available for cultural and scientific purposes.

Karen Blixen left for the United States on January 2, 1959.—The idea
of such a visit had been brought up several times but it did not materialize until Dr. Alvin C. Eurich, of the Fund for the Advancement
of Education, under the Ford Foundation, suggested that a television
show be produced with Karen Blixen talking about her work and reading from her books—actually, she preferred to recite from memory and
did so in this particular instance too. More invitations followed: one
to be the guest of honor at the annual dinner of the American Academy
and the National Institute, where she was expected to deliver a speech
or lecture; another from the Institute of Contemporary Arts involving
obligations in Washington and Boston; and one invitation asking nothing whatever in return: the editors of the *Ladies' Home Journal*, who
had published many of her stories, invited her to stay for two weeks at
the distinguished Cosmopolitan Club in New York. All these activities proved to be too much for Karen Blixen; she was so exhausted that
the American doctors were afraid she might not even get back alive.
However, it was one of the happiest experiences she had in her later
years, and it was only reluctantly that she terminated the visit after
three and a half months and returned to Denmark on her birthday,
April 17. She was accompanied on the trip by her secretary, Clara
Svendsen (picture above).

Opposite page: one of the best-known portraits of Karen Blixen, taken
by Cecil Beaton in New York in 1959.

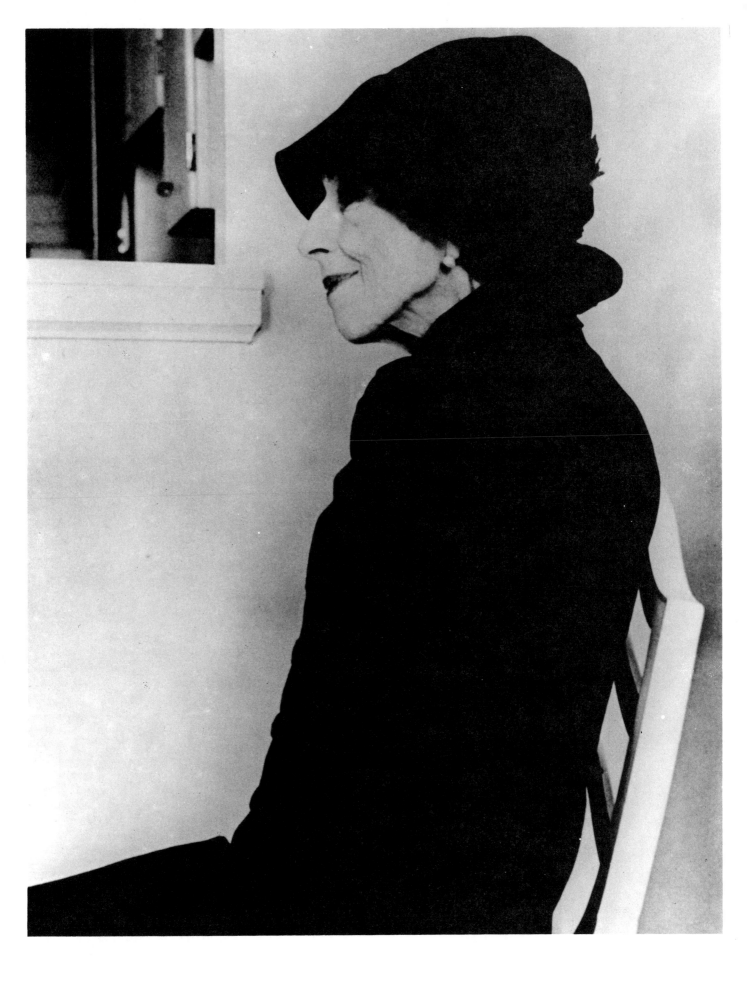

Arthur Miller, Marilyn Monroe, Carson McCullers and Karen Blixen in Carson McCullers' home in Nyack, January 1959. — At the dinner of the American Academy and the National Institute, to which she had been escorted by Glenway Wescott and E. E. Cummings, Karen Blixen had also met Arthur Miller and Carson McCullers, whose book *The Heart Is a Lonely Hunter* she liked very much. Carson McCullers, on her part, was very fond of *Out of Africa*, and as Karen Blixen was interested in meeting Marilyn Monroe, Carson McCullers invited the Millers and Karen Blixen to lunch in her home a few days later.

The two sisters Karen Blixen and Ellen Dahl at Rungstedlund in the late fifties. — When Karen Blixen left the C. A. Reitzel publishing house, whose owner was her brother-in-law Knud Dahl, and went to another publisher, there were certain disagreements, but some years later the tension had been relieved; Knud Dahl visited Karen Blixen at Rungstedlund several times before his death, and the two sisters became very close during the last ten years of Ellen Dahl's life. They would sometimes speak in "Pirogets," their and Ea's secret language of their childhood. Ellen Dahl preached to her sister, "One must resign oneself to the inevitable," but this was one thing Karen Blixen was incapable of doing. It was in the middle of the strenuous and eventful American visit, in February 1959 in Boston, that she received a telegram from Thomas Dinesen with the sad news of Ellen's death.

Above: Clara Svendsen's house in Dragør, the small seaport and fishing village on the island of Amager south of Copenhagen, where Karen Blixen stayed in the summer of 1960. —In the late fifties a decision had to be made whether Rungstedlund should be abandoned and demolished or completely modernized. The rebuilding of the house was carried out under the guidance of Professor Steen Eiler Rasmussen. Without a home for a longer period than anticipated, Karen Blixen accepted the invitation to come and live in the fisherman's cottage — only "two small rooms and an attic," just like Boganis' cottage in America—but she said right away, "Here you feel that you are in a real home." In this house she completed the Danish version of *Shadows on the Grass.*

Opposite page: 1960 was the international "Refugee Year" and Karen Blixen was actively engaged in the arrangements both in Hørsholm and in Dragør. In the photograph she is seen sending a letter by balloon from the harbor square in Dragør. Just before that she had told "The Blue Eyes," the story about a sailor, and had spoken of Dragør, which with its seafaring traditions would surely understand what it meant to have a home to return to—and not having one.

Tom Kristensen, Hans Brix and Karen Blixen on the day of the foundation of the Danish Academy.*—It had come into being on the initiative of, among others, Professor Christian Elling and the author Karl
Bjarnhof, and Karen Blixen had accepted the invitation to become a
charter member. After Karen Blixen's death, the main building at Rungstedlund was made available to the academy members, who hold their
meetings there and have guestrooms at their disposal.

*Tom Kristensen, novelist and poet, was one of the few Danish critics who appreciated
Seven Gothic Tales when it first appeared. Professor Hans Brix was the first to publish
a book about Karen Blixen (1949).

The portraits on pages 203, 204 and 205 were taken at Rungstedlund
by Peter H. Beard, who after having read *Out of Africa* while still in
school became more interested in Karen Blixen's Africa than in anything else.

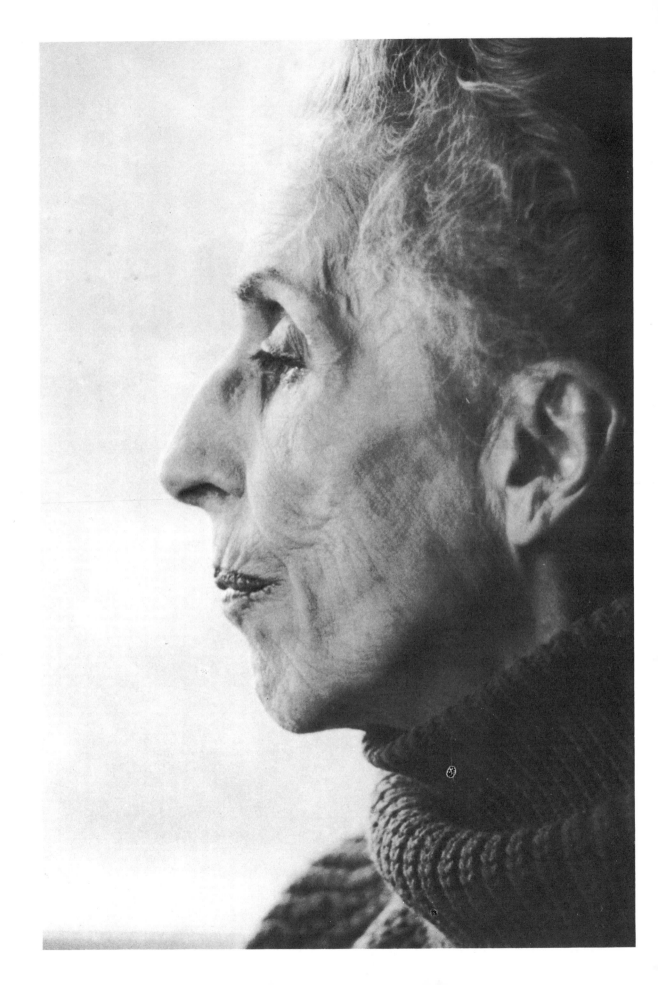

Not being a collector, Karen Blixen gave Thomas Dinesen some native shields and spears she had brought home from Africa. However, after the establishment of the Rungstedlund Foundation and the restoration of the house, she thought it would be suitable to have them in "Ewald's Room" and Thomas Dinesen obliged by presenting Rungstedlund with the weapons, which he put up on the north wall himself. He also donated to this small memorial room the two portraits of Africans, painted by Karen Blixen, which he owned.—Right up to 1960, the Louis XVI wood-burning stove from Norway was the only source of heat in this room.

Opposite page: The desk in "Ewald's Room," where Karen Blixen worked until the day before she lost consciousness.

The drawing room with flowers from the garden.—During the last years the garden was supervised by Ingwer Ingwersen, the horticulturist in charge of the garden of Rosenborg Castle. His mother had been one of the young Dinesen sisters' friends at Rungstedlund. In the summer of 1962 it cost Karen Blixen the greatest effort to walk as far as the flower garden, but she insisted on doing it, to select flowers for the rooms, and there was an abundance of them.

The dining room. Christel Jørgensen is laying the table for lunch. —
Many guests from Europe, America and Africa were seated at this
table during the last spring and summer. On April 17, hot chocolate
was traditionally served at the birthday party with relatives and friends.
Among them was one of Karen Blixen's oldest friends, Ellen Lassen,
née Wanscher, who all through her life signed her letters to Karen
Blixen with the name she had assumed in their childhood games.

The last spring.—Flanking Karen Blixen: Pepper, her last dog; Clara Svendsen; Nils Carlsen; Caroline Carlsen; and Christel Jørgensen, the last parlormaid at Rungstedlund.

Opposite page: Anders Dinesen and Karen Blixen outside Øregaard, May 1960.—One of the places Karen Blixen sometimes took her guests to see was Øregaard, the summer residence of her great-grandfather A. N. Hansen. During the last years of her life, when she was too weak to take the train to Copenhagen and instead made the trip by the local taxi with Helge or Asger Juul at the wheel, she would always have the car drive slowly past the house to enable her to have a lingering look at it.

The American edition of *Shadows on the Grass* was published in the beginning of 1961, and was a Book-of-the-Month Club choice. Shortly afterward Karen Blixen received an unofficial inquiry from *Life* magazine asking if she wanted to go to Kenya in their behalf; she replied that she would like to go down there to see those of her old people from the farm with whom she had contact and that the *Life* photographer was welcome to cover such an undertaking. Karen Blixen also wrote to a young member of the Blixen family who was farming in Kenya, and asked if there were any other Africans left who remembered her. He replied that he had met many, and one of them had told him, "We called her *"maua,"* because her heart was like a flower." Therefore, in her reply to *Life* she stated as her only special credential: "I am the only white person the natives really loved"—meaning of course in her own time and locality, a perhaps naïve but truthful statement, borne out later by other evidence. But when, in the summer of 1961, Karen Blixen sat in a Paris audience seeing Jack Gelber's *The Connection*, one of the characters, firing off disconnected silly sayings by white people about Negroes, suddenly quoted those words of hers. But she had become somewhat deaf in old age—for which her escorts were grateful.

The editors had a profusion of other plans and the trip to Kenya did not materialize. But in 1962 she received a visit which gave her great joy. Emma Wamboi Njonjo, a grandniece of the big chief Kinanjui, who plays such an important part in the book about the farm, had come to Denmark for further studies, and she wrote Karen Blixen that she had been asked by her father to convey his compliments. The gentle and graceful natural dignity of this very capable young woman was the most beautiful greeting Karen Blixen could ever have received from Africa (above).

Kamante Gaturra, the Kamante of *Out of Africa*, outside Karen Blixen's African house, photographed in 1961 by Peter H. Beard. Among the other photographs taken on this occasion was a portrait of Kamante which he himself sent to Karen Blixen, and it had its place on her desk during the last few months of her life.

Since the operations in 1955 ánd 1956, it had been a problem for Karen Blixen to take nourishment. All the most easily digestible foods were tried out, from oysters to nutrients in powder form dissolved in water, and in America they even tried to administer food to her through a plastic tube. In 1961 she was persuaded by friends to buy a vegetable and fruit juicer. It is not unlikely that this added a few extra months to her life, the happy and harmonious days of the spring and summer 1962.

During the summer of 1962 Karen Blixen liked to sit on the veranda on the north side of the house, facing the harbor. During the reconstruction in 1960 she had had a west window put in, to admit the afternoon sun. One of the many guests that year, an old friend, wrote to tell her how beautiful he had found everything around "your sunset," words that she treasured in serenity. She also said, "So many people complain about this summer. But it has been so lovely."

Overleaf: Karen Blixen had wished for a long time to add new pastures to the existing grassland at Rungstedlund, so that looking out of the windows in the guest apartment across the pond, one could see the cows grazing. With the help of her good friend Erik Kopp, Anne Dinesen's husband, the plan was realized in record time. In the picture on pages 216–17 she is happily and proudly inspecting the cows, as she had in former times by the dam she and Old Knudsen built on the African farm.

Right up to the end of August, Karen Blixen had visitors from Italy, France, England, Sweden and Norway. One of them was Cecil Beaton. They both knew that the pictures which were then taken (pages 214, 218 and 219) would be the last. In anticipation of his visit, Karen Blixen made one of her last flower arrangements, in a big tureen, placed on top of the brass-mounted chest given to her by Farah in Africa, and Cecil Beaton brought her one of the last bouquets she received from outside, flowers picked out from the ordinary selection of a small florist's and arranged into a marvelous little work of art.

In plenty of time—years before—Karen Blixen had quoted Landor's
lines during an interview:

"Nature I loved; and next to Nature, Art.
I warm'd both hands before the fire of life;
It sinks, and I am ready to depart."

Until the very end, Karen Blixen worked almost every day in "Ewald's Room" (photo below), dictating new stories, articles and forewords, rehearsing a reading to be recorded in English, answering letters and attending to business matters. On September 5 Karen Blixen signed her last contract (below, right). She also wrote a birthday letter in her own hand to her sister-in-law Jonna Dinesen, although it was not her birthday until the eighth, and said to her secretary, "It's important to get this off."

Rungstedlund, den 5. 9. 1962

Karen Blixen Finecke

In the evening of September 5, Karen Blixen listened to music on a new record player, a present from American friends. It was installed in the chest Farah had given her and which in Africa had served as a record cabinet. One of the records she listened to that evening was Händel's aria "Where'er You Walk," which Denys had sung to her. With difficulty and in great pain, as so often through the years and almost constantly during the last twelve months, she managed to climb the stairs to her bedroom in the east wing. She did not walk downstairs again; she died on September 7, at five o'clock in the afternoon.

The funeral service took place on September 11, at home, as had once her mother's, and was attended only by the family and her closest friends. Her last resting place was "under a big tree," as she had intended it years ago for Old Knudsen, under a big tree like the holy places of the Kikuyu in the African highland.—The arrangements were so plain, simple and private that it was easy to comply with a wish she had sometimes expressed that Schubert's "Frühlingsglaube" be sung at her funeral. This song, concluding in the line *"Nun muss sich alles, alles wenden,"* was sung in the home, and in accordance with her own wish, the ceremony at the grave included the reading of the Psalm beginning "I have lifted up my eyes to the mountains."

The road leading to the grave in the park at Rungstedlund.

The grave under the large beech tree at the foot of Ewald's Hill.

The house at Ngong came to be known as Karen House, and the new suburb which grew up around it was given the name of Karen. — But all that Karen Blixen herself owned of the soil of Africa at the time of her death was a handful she had brought back in a little wooden box. It was so arranged that those few grains of African earth were mixed with the soil of Zealand in her grave.

NAME INDEX

(Page numbers in italics refer to photographs)

In addition to the photographic reproductions of books and manuscripts provided by the Royal Library in Copenhagen, photographs by the following have been used in the book:

Anderson 64, Birthe Andrup 179, Peter E. Beard 203, 204, 205, 213, Cecil Beaton 197, 214, 218, 219, Pierre Boulat 191, 192, Joh Fr. Braae 35, Caroline Carlsen 199, Helge Christensen 224, Tage Christensen 177, 221, Thomas Dinesen 71, 79, 85, 86, 94, 95, 104, 106, 107, 109, 110, 112, 113, 114, 119, 120, 139, 147, Elfelt 19, 99, 100, 124, 140, 152, 153, 164, 194, 220, 222, 223, Denys Finch-Hatton 132, 137, Georg E. Hansen 24, 29, 34, Johannes Hansen 44, Kaj Lund Hansen 196, Jesper Høm 216–17 Knud W. Jensen 169, Juncker-Jensen 67, Peter Juul 173, Axel Jørgensen 36, Reimert Kehlet 145, Ove Kjeldsen 182, Olaf Kjelstrup 167, Frans Lasson 201, Jacob Maarbjerg 170, 202, Rie Nissen 153, 157, 180, 181, Børge Noer 212, Johannes Øvereng 163, Paetz 56, Per Pejstrup 195, J. Petersen 22, 36, N. E. Sinding 26, 30, Jane Sprague 183, John Stewart 206, 207, 208, 209, 210, 211, 215, Clara Svendsen 178, 188, 189, 190, 200, Carl Søgaard 127.

Most of the early photographers remain unidentified.

Karen Blixen's handwriting on page 7 reproduces a sentence from one of the early tales, "Eneboerne" (The Hermits), printed in *Tilskueren* (1907).

For the following captions unpublished sources have been drawn upon.

Oral information:

Karen Blixen: pp. 26, 27, 28, 32, 33, 34, 35, 40, 42, 43, 44, 50, 54, 55, 56, 65, 66, 72, 73, 74, 77, 78, 83, 84, 85, 87, 88, 92, 97, 98, 104, 108, 109, 112, 115, 116, 118, 122, 128, 131, 135, 136, 141, 142, 144, 148, 149, 150, 153, 154, 158, 161, 172, 174, 175, 176, 182, 189, 220
Dr. Henry Aranow: 196
Mrs. Christine Clemmesen: 138, 139
Thomas Dinesen: 16, 71, 79
Mrs. Robert K. Haas: 144
Mrs. Helene Landgren: 66
Gerda Hertel Wulff: 166

Unpublished written sources:

Karen Blixen: 68, 77, 122, 126
Abdullahi Ahamed: 101
Thomas Dinesen: 54, 101
Johannes V. Jensen: 151
Kamante Gaturra: 114
Franz Rohr: 156
Gustaf Blixen Finecke: 198

C.S.